STAND UP TO YOUR STOCKBROKER

STAND UP TO YOUR STOCKBROKER

Your Rights As an Investor

SANFORD S. KANTOR

AND

JOEL H. BERNSTEIN

WITH

DAVID W. KENNEDY

and the Editors of

Consumer Reports Books

CONSUMER REPORTS BOOKS

A Division of Consumers Union
Yonkers, New York

Library of Congress Cataloging-in-Publication Data
Kantor, Sanford S.
    Stand up to your stockbroker : your rights as an investor /
Sanford S. Kantor and Joel H. Bernstein with David W. Kennedy and
the editors of Consumer Reports Books.
        p. cm.
    Includes bibliographical references and index.
    ISBN 0-89043-347-X. — ISBN 0-89043-346-1 (pbk.)
    1. Investments. 2. Investment advisers. I. Bernstein, Joel H.,
    1949–   . II. Kennedy, David W. III. Consumer Reports Books.
    IV. Title.
    HG4521.K27   1991
    332.6—dc20   90-20535
                                                                      CIP
                                                                      Rev.

Design by Joy Taylor

First printing, March 1991
Manufactured in the United States of America

CONTENTS

ACKNOWLEDGMENTS

The authors gratefully acknowledge the impetus of Carl Altman in creating this book and in bringing it to fruition. His foresight and creative abilities have been an ongoing inspiration to our continuing mission to protect the investing public and to inform consumers of their rights.

We also thank Roslyn Siegel, our editor at Consumer Reports Books, for giving us the necessary guidance and direction to best present this information.

INTRODUCTION

Anthony Mancuso,* a hardworking and successful plumber, gave up college to build his father's business into one of the most respected operations in the county. He was a highly regarded businessman. When it came to buying plumbing supplies and equipment, he carefully researched and investigated all his options.

His investments were bank-oriented: money market accounts, certificates of deposit, life insurance—all simple and safe. His two forays into the stock market were based on "hot tips"— one from a friend, the other from a trusted business acquaintance. One stock went down, then up, enabling him to make a modest profit, and he sold it. His second stock purchase doubled in value in three months.

About six months after his last buy-and-sell adventure, the phone rang one evening:

"Mr. Mancuso, this is Vince McDonald. How are you?"

Anthony couldn't place the name. Was this a customer, a contractor, or maybe one of his daughter's boyfriends? "Do I know you?" he asked.

---

*All names in this book have been changed. The scenarios presented are fictional, but the situations are all too typical.

A baritone voice responded. "This is Vince McDonald from Adams, Adams, and Wilson. I'm sure you've heard of us before. We are a securities firm specializing in new issues. Our company sponsors growing corporations with excellent potential for future profits. Such companies require outside investment support to allow that expansion to take place. In other words, we create new issues and take these companies 'public.' We have one of the best reputations in the business as general brokers."

"Frankly, Vince, I haven't heard of you or your company," said Anthony.

"We have a number of prominent businessmen and leaders in the community who work with us, Anthony." Vince reeled off a list of names, some of whom Anthony knew. Anthony was impressed.

"The reason I called you tonight, Anthony, is that I'm contacting a number of successful people such as yourself to see if you would be interested in some new opportunities that I'm presently developing. The growth of new industries in this county is considerable, and some of the products being distributed have dynamic profit potentials. As a matter of fact, I will be meeting with the management of an environmental product manufacturer who recently secured patents on their process. I'll be seeing them next week, and if you would like, I can call you back and let you know if we think there's anything worth pursuing."

Anthony was flattered. He was being given the opportunity to get in on the ground floor. He decided that it couldn't hurt to hear what Vince would report back, so he said, "Sure, give me a call when you have more facts."

Two weeks later, Vince called, cautiously enthusiastic. Based on the discussions he'd had with the management of the environmental company, there was an exciting opportunity with the firm.

Vince projected sincere caution: "Anthony, it's very important that our team of marketing and financial experts analyze the structure of this company and accurately forecast the demand for the product they want to manufacture. Additionally, there are some environmental consultants whom we have worked with in the past, and we want to run this by them. I'll call you back next Tuesday and bring you up to date, all right?"

"Fine," said Anthony, thinking, This Vince is no slouch. He's doing things the right way. Anthony looked forward to hearing from him again.

When Vince called back on Tuesday, he was primed for the kill. He had patiently baited the trap for the previous month. He established credibility by naming known businessmen in the community, and Anthony Mancuso hadn't bothered to check them out. He constructed his offering around a "glamour industry" that had received considerable media coverage. The hook was set, and all that remained was to reel in the catch.

"Mr. Mancuso, this is Vince McDonald from Adams, Adams, and Wilson. My company has completed its findings and has decided to sponsor a new issue. It's even better than we expected, and it's a definite go! The market for this type of environmental product is wide open. The offering will be at $2 a share and all of our clients are gobbling it up. My allotment of shares will be gone by the end of the week. I've reserved 10,000 shares for you. Can you send me a check for $20,000 tomorrow?"

Anthony said yes.

"That's wonderful. As soon as I receive your check, I'll send you a customer's agreement and we'll follow up with the stock certificates when they're issued. Thank you very much, Anthony, and call me to check on the progress we're making."

No customer's agreement came in the mail, nor did a confirmation of receipt of the check. Anthony called the phone number Vince had given him, only to hear a disconnect recording. The telephone directory had no listing for Adams, Adams, and Wilson. And yes, the bank had cleared his check.

Anthony Mancuso was far from being the only person swindled out of significant sums of money in the United States last year. Allowing for variations on a theme, thousands of inexperienced investors can tell you the same story. They extended their trust without knowing the basic rules of buying securities.

Had he been buying a bathroom sink from a new supplier, Anthony Mancuso would have researched both the product and the vendor ten times over. He would have checked trade references, examined the terms of the sale, and obtained a Dun and Bradstreet report to confirm the reliability of the firm.

But, in an area he knew little about, Anthony Mancuso acted blindly. This book should keep such things from happening to you, and it should provide you with weapons to use if a brokerage or investment firm tries to take advantage of you.

The purpose of *Stand Up to Your Stockbroker* goes well beyond the goal of protecting the inexperienced or naïve investor against outright fraud. The authors of this book are attorneys specializing in securities fraud. Our practice is dominated by investors who seek recourse because they feel someone has taken advantage of them. In this book we will examine what constitutes the legal rights of investors, how the markets function, and the responsibilities that brokers and salespeople in this industry must fulfill. Our purposes are to make investors aware of the abuses that frequently occur, to help investors protect themselves, and to help them understand the avenues of recourse that can be used if problems arise.

1· THE INVESTMENT MARKETPLACE

To many people, including experienced investors, the American investment scene is a maze of products and possibilities. You can choose from an enormous array of stocks, bonds, mutual funds, limited partnerships, metals, real estate, commodities, options, and other products of all kinds. Which one should you pick? Which investment will help you achieve your financial goals? Which one takes into account your particular tolerance for risk? The average investor is overwhelmed and usually seeks expert guidance from financial professionals known as brokers, who, besides offering financial advice, sell these products to investors.

Why Invest?

So why should you invest at all? If you are not careful—and even if you are—you could lose your money. The question has two answers. The first is that only by investing wisely and well can most people reach their financial goals. Too often, people spend everything they earn and have nothing left over to meet

1

their long-range financial objectives, such as purchasing a home or sending their children to college. Investing offers the possibility of a second source of funds. While you work at one job, your money is working at another.

The second answer can be summed up in one word—**inflation**. Inflation is defined as a general rise in the price of goods and services over a period of time. This could be the increase in the cost of a quart of milk from 75 cents to 78 cents a week later, or a car from $15,000 to $15,500. So the dollar you earned today is worth less than the dollar you earned·a week ago. It becomes a cumulative process: This year's dollar is worth less than last year's and, if inflation continues, next year's dollar will be worth less than this year's. Unless your income rises at the same rate as inflation, you will be unable to keep up with prices.

Inflation occurs to some extent almost constantly. The U.S. government tracks inflation annually, and it is common for prices to rise 3 to 4 percent a year. (For a time in the 1970s, inflation was running at 10 to 12 percent per year.) If you put your money into a savings account that pays 5½ percent interest, you are staying only about 1½ percent ahead of inflation. There are other instruments of investment that do pay a higher interest. After you pay taxes on the interest you earn, you'll be lucky if you're even with inflation! And if inflation rises to, say, 6 or 7 percent, you will be losing money on your savings. Investing, then, is an effort to stay ahead of inflation by attaining a return significantly higher than inflation. At present, 8 to 10 percent is a reasonable target.

The Market Transaction

Securities are issued by corporations, municipalities, or government agencies for one reason—to raise money. A corporation, for example, may want to build a new manufacturing facility but doesn't want to borrow any more money from its bank, so it seeks an alternative, either issuing stock or floating (offering to the public) a bond issue. Or a city finds it necessary to build a new bridge but all of its tax revenues are already earmarked. So it issues bonds to finance the project. Stocks (ownership interest in a corporation), bonds (interest-bearing IOUs issued by a corporation or a branch of government), and options (contracts that involve the right to buy or sell something at a specified price within a certain time period) are all securities. It is the buyers of stocks and bonds who provide the money necessary to build the plant or bridge. It is this process of investing, with its constant raising of money, that helps the economy grow.

Anyone who wants to buy or sell a stock, bond, or option ordinarily must consummate that transaction through a registered representative who is affiliated with a firm known as a **broker-dealer**, more commonly called brokerage or securities firms. Any transaction, whether a purchase or a sale, is known as a **trade**.

Investors can also buy and sell gold, silver, and other strategic metals, along with wheat, pork bellies, and other agricultural products. These are called **commodities**. Commodities are highly specialized investments that are subject to different economic and financial forces from securities, and, as a result, are classified differently. Commodities, which are governed by their own rules and regulations, are bought or sold through **associated persons**, who work for futures commission merchants. Many large broker-dealers are also futures commission merchants, and your broker could be a registered representative *and* an associated person who can also trade commodities.

The Players

Every securities transaction involves three people: a buyer, a seller, and a broker who executes the trade. **Execution** means transferring the security from one person to another. All licensed brokers are capable of doing this. The broker is an individual who, for a commission, buys or sells securities or commodities on your behalf. You can be either a buyer or seller; in either case, you pay a commission to the broker for the execution of the trade.

Securities buyers and sellers can be brought together in various ways. Marketplaces, known as exchanges, have been established for the public trading of stocks and bonds. The best known of these are the **New York Stock Exchange (NYSE)** (the "Big Board") and the **American Stock Exchange (AMEX)**, both located in New York City. Most larger corporations deal on the NYSE, while the somewhat smaller ones trade on the AMEX. There are also a number of regional stock exchanges and specialized exchanges, such as the Midwest Stock Exchange in Chicago and the Pacific Stock Exchange in Los Angeles.

More than 3,000 stocks trade on these exchanges, but an even larger number trade "over-the-counter," through a decentralized, computer-assisted network of broker-dealers. Most small-company stocks trade over-the-counter.

Broker-Dealers

Broker-dealers, also known as brokerage firms or securities dealers, provide the support and supervision for the individual brokers who work for them. When a broker receives an order, the order usually is processed by that broker's firm. The firm must keep track of all the paperwork and is responsible if anything goes wrong. Some small broker-dealers do not process their own trades but instead engage another firm, known as a clearing broker, to do it for them. In that situation, the broker-dealer is subcontracting the paperwork, but it remains responsible if errors occur. The broker-dealer has a fiduciary duty toward the customer, just as its employee, the registered representative, does. This fiduciary duty requires that the financial interests of the consumer be protected above all else.

There are essentially three types of securities firms. The **full-service brokerage** offers a full range of products from stocks and bonds to options and commodities. It normally produces research opinions on many of those products that it may recommend to its clients, and of course it executes trades for its customers. The full-service broker-dealer may also develop and sell its own financial products, such as mutual funds, money market funds, limited partnerships, and other securities. Brokers who work for full-service firms earn most of their money from commissions, and customers usually pay a relatively high commission (from 3 to 5 percent) for all these services. If you are a frequent trader, you can usually get a reduced commission.

Discount brokerage firms charge lower commissions because they do little more than execute trades. Discounters usually charge either a set amount for each share traded or a percentage of the total value of the transaction. They normally don't offer any research or make recommendations, and their salespeople are on salary rather than on commission.

Specialized brokerages trade only some specific form of investment, such as commodities, penny stocks, or mutual funds. They may charge a full commission or a discounted price. They may offer research and make recommendations, but only on products relating to their specialty.

No matter what kind of broker-dealer you use, all are subject to the same rules and regulations with regard to customers and their accounts. Discount brokers owe their customers the same legal obligations owed by the full-service firms and the specialized broker-dealers.

Financial Supermarkets

Many of the large full-service firms now offer products and services in addition to securities trading. These include insurance, mortgages, credit cards, and checking accounts. Advertising themselves as one-stop financial shopping outlets, brokerage firms hope to handle all of a customer's financial business. This is convenient, but it could also be risky. For example, any stocks you own could become collateral for checking overdrafts and credit cards. Also, one organization may not perform all financial functions equally well. It usually is wiser to spread your business around.

Regulation of Broker-Dealers

Just like a bank that holds your money, the brokerage firm is highly regulated by the federal government. The government's primary interest is in seeing to it that the small investor is treated fairly and that if the investor loses money, it is because of risks associated with the marketplace, not with the investment firms themselves. (See chapter 9.)

Exchanges

In order for a broker-dealer to make a trade on the New York Stock Exchange or any of the other exchanges around the country, that firm must be admitted to membership on that exchange. Although technically a firm does not obtain membership—an individual does—the membership can be passed from one individual to another in a firm.

Members have "seats," which means they have the right to do business on the exchange premises. Although the actual exchange takes place on the premises, orders can be taken anywhere. Almost all full-service and most discount brokerage firms are members of one or more exchanges that handle their particular product, such as commodities.

Exchanges serve five main functions:

1. They provide an orderly marketplace for the trading of securities.
2. Through an auction process, they determine a fair price for both the buyer and the seller of securities.

3. They provide liquidity—that is, the ability to turn the asset into immediate cash—for sellers.

4. They provide a collection point and act as a reputable source of sales reporting and quotes for the general public.

5. They enforce certain regulations for the protection of buyers and sellers.

When a security is eligible to be traded on a particular exchange, it is said to be **listed** for trading. Once the security is listed, any exchange member can trade the security on that exchange. There are, however, a large number of securities that are unlisted, or are not traded on an exchange. These unlisted securities are instead traded in what is known as the **over-the-counter** market (OTC). OTC trades are not made in a particular exchange with a physical location but rather are traded over the phone or by computer. Almost all full-service and discount broker-dealers trade over-the-counter.

When you give a buy or sell order to your broker, that order is routed to the proper exchange or to the OTC and is executed. Execution occurs when your order is paired with that of someone who wants to buy or sell the same number of shares of the same security at the same price. All firms that are members of an exchange have an individual—or, more likely, a group of individuals—on the floor of the exchange during trading hours to make the actual trades. The **registered representative** who solicits the buy or sell order does not execute it; the floor broker does that. Whereas the representative gets a commission for a sale, the floor broker generally receives a salary.

2 · INVESTMENT RISKS

Investing is a risky enterprise. You won't always be right; sometimes you will lose money. Obviously, the idea is to keep your losses to a minimum. Successful investors try to minimize their losses by sticking to a coherent and consistent **investment philosophy** from which they build a portfolio.

Your Investment Philosophy

If you are like most people, your outlook changes as your circumstances change. If you are young, you are probably something of a risk taker. Married individuals usually take fewer risks than single people.

Similarly, your goals change. If your reason for investing is to purchase a home, you might adjust your philosophy to meet that goal. However, once you buy the home, your new goal might be to invest so you can send your children to college. Attaining that goal might again alter your philosophy, and your new goal might be to secure your retirement.

Your philosophy is always being stretched to meet the needs of your goals and adjustments, and fine-tuning of your investments will be necessary.

Your Portfolio

A **portfolio** is the collection of all of the securities in which you have invested at any one time. For instance, if you hold three different common stocks, a mutual fund, some corporate bonds, and a limited partnership, all of those securities constitute your portfolio.

Your portfolio will change as your needs and goals change. When you are young, investing in high-risk start-up companies may be more appropriate than when you are older and trying to save money for your child's education.

Six elements go into the construction of a portfolio:

1. Your age
2. Your financial goals
3. How many years left until you need to reach a particular financial goal
4. How much you can afford to invest
5. Your financial circumstances
6. How much risk you are willing to take

Once all these elements have been sorted out, appropriate investments can be selected to meet the criteria.

The Risks of Investing

If an investment you purchase decreases in value, that doesn't mean your broker is at fault. There are no foolproof investments. Savings banks once were thought to be a safe place for your money, but in recent years, some savings and loan associations (S&Ls) and other financial institutions have gone bankrupt and, in some cases, investors have lost their money.

However, some investments are safer than others under most circumstances. For example, U.S. government bonds—because they are essentially IOUs of the government of the United States—are considered much safer than the stock of a start-up company. Similarly, buying stock in an established corporation is less risky than buying pork bellies on the commodities exchange.

Market Risk

Securities are not sold in a vacuum; they are subject to a number of outside influences. There is a good deal of "investor psychology" involved in the upward-and-downward course of a market. It is uncertain what triggers that psychology and why stocks, for example, move in the direction they do. Even professional investors sometimes are fooled by the price movement of certain securities.

Often the market is up one day and down the next and continues going up and down in no discernible pattern. This is known as **market volatility**, and it is a normal, though sometimes annoying, phenomenon.

Worse, there are days when the vast majority of stocks decline, or even plunge, in price. Illness or assassination of a world leader, negative economic news, international hostilities, or a major corporate bankruptcy can do the trick. If your stock declines on such a day, it doesn't mean you're a poor stock picker. You are experiencing market risk.

Market risk, then, is essentially unrelated to the worth of an individual investment. No matter how good a security may appear to be, it can go down just as easily as it can go up, because it is subject to the vagaries of a trading market and investor psychology.

Risks of the Economy

Another risk over which you have no control is the condition of the American economy at any given time. Widely traded investments are subject, to a greater or lesser extent, to what is happening in the economy. If the economy is in the depths of a recession, the chances are that several kinds of investments, particularly stocks, will return less than if the economy were booming.

Interest-Rate Risk

Economic events constantly affect investment strategies. For example, the interest rate that bonds pay can vary. One-year bonds may average a 9 percent rate of return, while two years later, rates may have jumped to 11 percent or fallen to 7 percent. Because of this, bonds are known as interest-sensitive investments.

You and your financial adviser must be aware of interest rates and economic conditions and be able to make educated guesses about alternative investment possibilities. Is it better, for example, to lock in a known interest rate on a bond or take a chance on a common-stock investment that may have a higher return? It's the need for this kind of analysis that prompts many investors to seek the services of an investment adviser.

The Financial Pyramid

Some experts use a **financial pyramid** to illustrate what they believe to be the proper mix of investments in a diversified portfolio. Imagine a typical pyramid, which is broad at the base and gradually works its way up to a point. At the bottom, the greatest percentage of your assets is in safe, liquid instruments such as cash and money market funds. Higher up on the pyramid would be government bonds that are guaranteed but may fluctuate in value over time. The next step contains vehicles that, for the most part, provide income and long-term growth; common stocks are the prime example. At the very top could be a small investment in more speculative products. Here you hope for higher returns but realize that there may well be a decline in value.

This pyramid offers a conservative, although not foolproof, method of investing that has gained wide acceptance. It puts a premium on safety. The majority of investors using this approach may not become wealthy, but they will not go broke either.

Get It in Writing

Some brokers tend to gloss over the risks of an investment because they are afraid of scaring you off and not making a sale; customers tend not to read the legal language in prospectuses and disclosure statements because they don't understand it. Both of those actions are mistakes. The broker who doesn't spell out the risks of a recommended security is leaving himself or herself open to a violation of the securities laws, and the customer runs the risk of losing his entire investment—or, in some cases, even *more* than the amount invested.

Don't be embarrassed or reticent about asking questions. If you are in any doubt about the characteristics and risks of an investment, ask your broker for a *written* explanation of it. The explanation should include reasons why the security is being recommended, risks associated with the security, and any limitations that might be involved. Limitations include whether or not a bond is **callable** (see Glossary), or, in the case of a convertible security, whether there is a time limit on the conversion privilege. A list of commissions and charges should also be included.

By demanding it in writing, you present yourself as a serious and careful investor, and the chances are that the broker will not try to take advantage of you. In addition, a written recommendation can be used as evidence if a dispute later arises over the transaction. If the registered representative will not give you a written recommendation, that is ample cause to consider taking your business elsewhere.

Investing Goals

How you invest is influenced by your reason for investing—to buy a house, to provide a nest egg for retirement, to send the kids to college. Your investing goal and the time you have available to reach that goal can make one investment preferable to another. If your goal is to send your eight- and ten-year-old children to college, time is short. You should be conservative, because you don't want to lose the money you have already put away for the kids' education. Instead of buying a limited partnership that might return 12 percent a year, you might buy some highly rated corporate bonds that yield a more certain 9 percent annually.

Investors' goals are often reduced to one-word descriptions by investment professionals. For example, a retired person investing to supplement his income will invest in bonds and certificates of deposit, which pay a steady income and also are safe. He is investing for **income**. The much younger investor who is looking for appreciation would be characterized as a **growth** investor. She would take some chances that the income investor wouldn't. Fundamentally, income investors are conservative and risk-averse, while growth investors are willing to shoulder more risk.

Diversification

You dramatically increase your risks by not diversifying funds among different types of investments. Putting all your available money into one type of investment is foolish. The idea behind **diversification** is that if one investment is not doing well, the others may make up for it. For example, stocks and bonds sometimes move in opposite directions: When stocks are generally doing well, bonds may be down, and vice versa. In the past two or three years, they usually have moved in the same direction. One reason: Falling interest rates are good for both. The financial pyramid is one example of diversification.

One of the big problems in investing is determining how to allocate your money among all the available investment possibilities. This decision-making process is called **asset allocation**. It is at this point that many investors seek the advice of a financial professional.

Your Experience As an Investor

If you are an experienced investor, you have learned something about the pitfalls of investing. You have learned about the benefits of diversification and you may know where to look for investments that fit your risk profile. However, just because you are experienced, don't assume that you can't be victimized by a broker. Experienced investors sometimes have a complacency that plays right into the hands of the larcenous or incompetent broker.

Take Charlie Hunter. He had been investing for twenty years, but his experience and knowledge of the financial markets was limited to taking his broker's advice. When that broker retired, Hunter was assigned to a new one. Hunter's father died and left Charlie $80,000 in cash. Charlie wanted to invest it with the goal of buying a franchise that he had been considering for some time.

Charlie's new broker talked him into putting the entire amount into "high-yield corporate bonds," which had an expected return of around 13 percent. The problem was that Charlie was not told about the great risks associated with these bonds—he was not informed that "high yield" is synonymous with **junk bonds**. The broker told Charlie that in addition to being high yield, these bonds were "highly rated," and that his firm's research department had a favorable opinion of them. That was not true. Charlie failed to ask for a copy of that opinion, nor did he check the rating on the bonds. He just took the broker at his word. When the corporation that issued the bonds defaulted on them, Charlie lost his entire investment.

Your Risk Profile

Your own **risk profile** involves many things—your attitude toward risk generally, how the trading markets are performing when you want to invest, the state of the economy, your goals for investing, and your experience as an investor. All of these factors must be evaluated constantly, and possibly adjusted as time goes on. The essence of investing is the interplay of all the known risks and opportunities, your goals, and what you can afford.

Taxes and Your Investments

For many years, the tax law has contained a concept that applies to securities, called **capital gains**. A capital gain is a profit on the sale of an asset, such as a stock or a bond. Such gains were for a long time taxed at a lower rate than ordinary income in order to encourage investments, but this no longer is the case. Since capital-gains tax laws change and interest made on stocks and bonds may be subject to several kinds of taxes, your registered representative must be sensitive to your particular tax situation.

Broker-Dealer Responsibilities

In order for the Internal Revenue Service to have an accurate record of how much taxable interest or dividends you have earned in a given year, your broker-dealer must report this information to the IRS. And to help you complete your tax return properly and accurately, your broker-dealer must send you a 1099 form indicating the exact amount of taxable interest and dividends you earned during the year.

In addition, if you sold securities or redeemed shares of a mutual fund, that information is reported to the IRS. The broker-dealer must send you a 1099B form that indicates the gross proceeds of those sales.

This is one of those jobs that the broker-dealer must perform with unerring accuracy. You should, of course, reconcile your records with those of the brokerage firm when you receive the 1099, and bring any discrepancies immediately to the attention of the firm's manager. In short, all activity in your account is disclosed to the IRS, and you must receive a copy of all the data for your records.

Tax Shelters

Prior to the Tax Reform Act of 1986, many limited partnerships were sold as tax shelters. That is, if you purchased such a partnership, you could often write off two or three times the amount of your investment on your taxes. For example, if you spent $5,000 for a partnership unit, you could deduct, possibly over a two-year period, $10,000. However, Congress put an end to these practices in 1986.

There are a few limited partnerships that still provide tax credits for investors: They are in the areas of historic rehabilitation and low-income housing. The amount of the credit is limited and depends on your income. Large brokerage firms often sell these credit partnerships through their registered reps. These may be legitimate investments, but you will need to evaluate their appropriateness for your portfolio.

Summing Up

Any investment professional (such as a stockbroker) who works with you should be keenly aware of all the factors discussed in this chapter. These include your age, your investment goals, your risk tolerance, and your tax situation. It is the broker's job to match your needs and your risk profile with the appropriate investments. A broker has a legal duty to "know the customer." The broker who knows you best will serve you best. However, it is *your* responsibility to make sure that the broker knows you and serves you.

3 · INVESTMENT PRODUCTS

Every investment product has its own characteristic features that you should take into consideration before investing. In other words, you should know its risk-and-reward profile. Among the questions you should ask are:

- For what purpose is the money being raised?
- Is the investment a volatile one?
- Do its price and its value tend to change quickly over a short period of time?
- Does it provide a dividend or pay interest, and, if so, how much?
- What are the short- and long-term outlooks for the company or governmental unit?
- If a stock, what is its price/earnings ratio and its earnings per share?
- How much debt does the issuer have?

The **price/earnings ratio** (P/E) is the current price of a stock divided by its earnings per share. Usually the past twelve months' earnings are used. Sometimes analysts use estimated earnings for the current year, or even for the coming year.

Earnings per share is simply a company's earnings (profits) after taxes, divided by the number of shares of common stock the company has issued.

The P/E is a measure of a stock's popularity and of investor optimism about a company's prospects. When investors expect earnings to grow rapidly, they are willing to pay more for each dollar of current earnings. Young, fast-growing companies have higher P/E ratios than older "blue-chip" companies.

It is surprising how many investors buy a product knowing little about its risk, what kinds of returns can be expected, and generally how the investment works. Remember that *no investment is without risk,* and no guarantees can or should be made in that regard. But knowledge of any security's risk profile can be a helpful guide in choosing your investments. Below is a brief summary of the various types of investment products and the important characteristics of each.

Common stock is the most widely held type of single security. When you buy common stock, you are buying a part-ownership voting interest in a company. Common stockholders vote for the board of directors, who hire the management and are generally responsible for the overall direction of the company. If the company is successful, and if the board of directors orders it, a dividend will be paid to stockholders. The dividend is paid out of profits earned by the company. In some situations, however, a dividend may not be paid. If the company is not doing well, the board may decide to omit a dividend and to pour profits back into the company. Or profits might be poured back to boost research and development that might result in greater appreciation later. The amount of the dividend and the value of the shares themselves can and frequently do fluctuate, depending on the fortunes of the company. In the case of a start-up company, dividends are infrequent. Investors are betting on a substantial appreciation in the value of the stock so that they can sell it later at a profit; thus, they are less concerned about immediate dividends.

There is no one risk profile for common stock. Investors who buy **blue-chip stocks**—that is, stocks of well-known, well-established corporations with a track record of profitability and dividend payment—generally are taking less of a risk than those who invest in a new issue of a start-up corporation. Nevertheless, it is necessary to evaluate each common-stock purchase in relation to the prevailing economic and financial circumstances. These include the growth of the gross national product as well as interest rates and unemployment.

If you buy **preferred stock**, you are still buying an ownership interest in a company, but it is an interest that may carry no voting rights. It is also characterized by the fact that the dividend (if there is one) is often fixed at a set rate and does not vary, as it can with common stock. Because preferred stockholders usually know what their dividend will be when they buy, they probably have a more conservative outlook than common stockholders and are less willing to take chances on what the dividend payout will be. For the same reason, preferred stock normally trades in a smaller price range and is not subject to the volatile price changes that occur with common stock. In the event of insolvency of the company issuing the stock, preferred stockholders are paid before common stockholders (hence the term *preferred*). Although preferred stock is not as well known to the general public as common stock, many companies issue both types. Few individuals buy preferred stock; it is bought mainly by corporations, which seek certain tax advantages from it.

Bonds are *debt securities* because they are debts of the corporation or governmental agency issuing them. When you purchase a bond, you are, in effect, lending money to the bond issuer. Because you have loaned money, you become a creditor of the issuer. As a creditor, a bondholder *must* be paid before common and preferred stockholders. Just as a bank earns interest on the loans it makes, so does the bond purchaser. Bonds normally have a fixed interest rate, and they usually are issued for a specified number of years. For example, if you bought a ten-year, 10 percent bond at a price of $1,000, you could expect to earn $100 a year in interest. If you still hold the bond when the ten-year term expires, the issuer will return your $1,000. In this case, over the ten years, you ultimately receive $2,000 for your $1,000 investment. Yield plus capital gain (or loss) is your total return.

The interest rate on bonds is generally higher than the rate at your bank. A drawback, however, is that your money is tied up for a considerable amount of time. In addition, the value of a bond changes with economic conditions. If you sell it before the ten years are up, you may get more or less than the $1,000 you paid for it.

Also, some bonds are callable before their term is up. This means that the issuer can redeem the bond (buy it back from you at a predetermined price). Depending upon that call price, an investor may lose money on his or her investment. In addition, if a bond is called when interest rates are lower than when the bond was issued, there will be a loss of anticipated income.

A call can turn into a real disaster if you paid more than the face amount for your bond (*buying at a premium*). In that instance, a call can mean a large capital loss. By now, you get the message: Before buying any bond, carefully discuss its call provisions with your broker or financial adviser.

There are various types of bonds. Bonds issued by a corporation are known as **corporate bonds.** The stronger the financial condition of the company, the less risky the bond. Generally speaking, risky bonds pay higher interest rates than safer bonds do—they *have* to, in order to attract investors. Corporate bonds that are *secured* are supported by collateral—property such as real estate or equipment owned by the company. However, some bonds are issued just on the good name and creditworthiness of the company. Such bonds are known as **debentures.**

Bonds run the entire gamut of the risk spectrum. High-grade

bonds (that is, those rated AAA by rating agencies such as Standard & Poor's or Moody's) issued by blue-chip corporations yield less but are safer than "junk bonds," which carry a much higher interest rate.

States, cities, and local governmental authorities also issue debt securities, called **municipal bonds.** Even though their interest rates are almost always lower than those of corporate bonds, a big advantage is that the interest earned is in many cases exempt from federal or state taxation or both. States and municipalities pay off their bonds (a process known as *debt service*) through tax revenues.

The federal government also raises money by issuing debt securities. The long-term ones, called **Treasury bonds,** are considered the safest of all bond types. Treasury bonds are exempt from state and local taxes, but not federal taxes. Shorter-term debt securities issued by the U.S. Treasury are called *Treasury notes* (one-year to ten-year maturities) and *Treasury bills.*

Convertible bonds can be exchanged for a set number of shares of common stock at a predetermined price. For example, a convertible bond could be convertible into 100 shares of common stock of the same company that issued the bond within five years of purchase at $20 a share. Convertible bonds earn a lower interest rate than regular bonds, but they offer the possibility of greater gains if the issuing company thrives.

Mutual funds are investment pools established and managed by investment companies. The managers buy a diversified portfolio of securities (it could be all stocks, all bonds, all options, or any combination) and the mutual-fund buyer then purchases a share of the entire portfolio. If the portfolio does well, so do the investors. Losses are also shared among the investors. The risk of mutual funds can be properly assessed only by looking at the securities that make up the fund. A mutual fund consisting of only newly issued stock of start-up companies will be significantly riskier, for example, than one made up of blue chips. A corporate or municipal bond fund, on the other hand, may be less or more risky than an equity fund, depending on the makeup of the fund's portfolio.

Mutual funds are classified according to the way you pay for them. The basic fees associated with a mutual fund are called the **load**. In a *no-load fund*, there is no up-front fee. If you invest $1,000 in a no-load fund, the entire $1,000 will go into purchasing shares of the fund. You will, however, have to pay an annual maintenance fee—typically, 1 percent of the value of the account.

If a mutual fund does have a load, that fee will be taken right off the top when you buy the fund and will be used mainly to pay a commission to the individual who sells the fund. Eight percent loads normally are the maximum charged. With an 8 percent load, for every $1,000 invested, $920 goes toward the purchase of fund shares while $80 goes for commissions and other expenses. There are also some low-load funds that carry a load of 3 or 4 percent as well as a yearly maintenance fee.

Some funds assess a fee for sales and marketing costs. Such fees, imposed annually, are called 12b-1 fees. Like other fees, they reduce the overall return from the investment.

Many mutual funds also charge a *back-end load* when you sell your shares in the fund. The amount of that fee varies with the fund.

Don't be misled. All mutual funds, whether or not they call themselves no load, will charge certain fees to the buyers of shares. The differences lie in the magnitude of the fees and in the timing of the charges.

Investors who are considering buying mutual funds must have an accurate picture of what costs are involved before deciding whether to choose a no-load or a load product. When calculating returns from a mutual-fund investment, you must take into consideration all the expenses—front-end load, annual fees, and back-end load. All of these costs and expenses must be detailed in the prospectus that every mutual-fund investor receives at the time of making the investment. The Securities and Exchange Commission (SEC) recently required that this information be presented in a standardized format, making it fairly easy to compare various funds' expenses.

Mortgage pass-through securities. Two quasi-governmental agencies, the **Government National Mortgage Association (GNMA)** and the **Federal National Mortgage Association (FNMA)**, issue popular securities nicknamed, respectively, Ginnie Maes and Fannie Maes. These agencies purchase VA- and FHA-guaranteed mortgages from banks and mortgage brokers and pool them into securities. The mortgages stand as collateral for the funds.

The payments that are made on the mortgages are passed through from the originating bank or savings-and-loan institution to the agencies. Investors receive the monthly principal and interest payments from these mortgages. These payments are not guaranteed by the federal government, as a whole, but rather by the agencies. Of the hundreds of individual homeowners whose mortgages make up the fund, a few are refinancing or selling their homes every month, causing the mortgages to be prepaid. Thus, the yield is liable to change monthly. These securities may be unsuitable if you are looking for a constant, predictable source of income.

Money market funds are mutual funds that invest in what is known as the money market. The money market is a market in which dealers for corporations, banks, and other institutions trade short-term debt securities (with maturities of one year or less) such as commercial paper issued by corporations and Treasury bills. Other short-term instruments traded on the money market include negotiable certificates of deposit and bankers acceptances.

Many money market funds purchase instruments issued by governments, the highest-rated corporations, and the world's largest banks. Some purchase the debt of original issuers, but even here, the short-term nature of the debt makes the funds less risky than most other types of investments. The money market is quite active, and the managers are constantly buying and selling money market instruments to maximize the return on the fund. The return on money market funds is modest (now from 7 to 8 percent in most cases) compared to other investments, because of the low risk involved. As a result, many investors use money market funds as a temporary parking place for their money until they decide on further investments.

Unit investment trusts are similar to mutual funds, but these investments are comprised of a fixed and unchanging portfolio of securities. Managers of mutual funds can alter the portfolio as economic and market conditions change. This cannot be done with a unit investment trust. When you buy into this investment, you know exactly what securities are involved and you know that they will not change. Unit investment trusts have a known return and you must pay a load to buy in.

Limited partnerships. A group of people pool their money and become partners in a business enterprise. The pooled money is used to purchase something tangible, such as an apartment complex, an oil or gas well, or a fleet of planes that are leased out. Many partnerships were structured as tax shelters prior to the changes made in the federal tax laws in 1986. Partnership success—or failure—depends on an individual or a small group called the general partner(s).

Because partnerships are difficult for the average investor to understand and evaluate, they have become a prime source of fraudulent activities in recent years. Even legitimate partnerships often carry extremely high fees that enrich the general partner while diluting the potential returns of the investors (limited partners).

Possible conflicts of interest also deserve careful scrutiny.

Some real-estate developers, for example, have retained their best properties and unloaded their less desirable properties into a limited partnership.

Before investing in a partnership, you should seek out a second opinion from an independent investment expert who is unconnected with the person who is trying to sell you a partnership.

Among the considerations the investor must keep in mind before investing in a partnership are:

1. The track record of the general partner
2. The type of partnership—i.e., real estate, oil and gas, or equipment leasing
3. The outlook for the particular industry under consideration, as well as the economy as a whole
4. The fees involved, which often are prohibitive
5. The possible lack of liquidity of the partnership units

Fees of 20 to 25 percent of your initial investment, including an 8 percent commission to the broker, are not uncommon. Some of the fees go for organization and offering expenses as well as acquisition costs. Some may go to ensure a quick profit for the general partners. Therefore, if you invest $5,000 in a limited partnership unit, less than $4,000 will go into the investment. While these fees are high, they are for the most part front-end fees; there are typically no annual maintenance charges or back-end loads in partnerships. There may be, however, a series of promissory notes or payments that must be made years into the future, even if the deal falls apart. That, in fact, is what happened to Kenny Ponte. His broker never told him that he might be required to make some more payments long after he had originally invested. Kenny was forced to cough up another $10,000, even though his partnership had never returned anything to him—and might never do so.

Partnerships have other drawbacks. In general, they are long-term investments, held for seven to ten years before you receive full value for your investment. Most partnerships do provide for a periodic return (called cash flow) similar to a dividend, but there are no guarantees that a return will be forthcoming. If you must sell the partnership prior to maturity, you can expect to incur a large loss, possibly 40 percent or more of your original investment. This is because partnership units (with the exception of a small group of partnerships known as master limited partnerships) are not traded on any stock exchange, so it can be difficult to find another willing buyer.

There are two types of limited partnership offerings. A public offering is open to anyone who meets a fairly minimal net-worth and income standard. Most average investors or members of the general public (hence the term *public offering*) qualify. A public partnership unit costs as little as $1,000, but a minimum investment of $5,000 is common. Private offerings—or, as they are routinely called, private placements—can by law be sold only to wealthier investors who meet more stringent net-worth and income standards. Typically, the minimum investment is much higher for buying into a private placement than for a public offering.

Many limited partnerships are sold by specialized firms that do little else. But several of the very large, well-known broker-dealers also cosponsor or act as co–general partners on limited partnership deals. In those cases, their own brokers may be the exclusive sales force for the product.

Commodities and futures. Commodities include such products as metals, heating oil, wheat, corn, pork bellies (bacon), orange juice, and other agricultural goods. Investing in a commodity involves betting on its future price. A commodity contract stipulates that a seller of the commodity will deliver a specific quantity to the buyer at a designated place at an agreed-upon price at a set date in the future. **Commodity futures** is another name given to this kind of transaction.

Futures transactions are also available in gold, silver, platinum, plywood, and rubber. There are also **financial futures,** involving the trading of foreign currencies, financial indexes such as the Standard & Poor's 500, and U.S. Treasury bonds. Some full-service broker-dealers trade commodities for interested clients, but, for the most part, specialized brokerages handle trades in this market.

In all of these investments, the buyer and the seller are trading on their belief in the future price of the product—which requires a significant amount of sophisticated analysis. The individual investor is matching wits with firms that have in-depth knowledge and up-to-the-minute information on a particular commodity. But that's the least of the investor's troubles.

Because the contract has a definite ending date, the investor must guess not only *what's* going to happen, but also *when* it's going to happen. That's doubly hard.

The commodities exchanges have been hit by periodic scandals. In 1989, the FBI had some of its agents pose as commodity traders. The government has charged several traders with cheating customers by charging them higher prices than necessary on purchases, or giving them lower prices than necessary on sales. While trials were still pending at this writing, the FBI sting was only the latest of several episodes that have scared many investors away from the commodity pits.

Commodity investing typically is done by making only a small good-faith deposit on a contract. This small sum controls a much larger sum in the commodity contract. As traders say, there's a lot of leverage. As a result, gains and losses are greatly magnified. It's common for a speculator to make much more than the money initially put up, but it's also common to lose much more than the amount invested. That, too, makes commodities one of the riskiest investments.

Finally, survey after survey has shown that the vast majority of commodities speculators lose money. For all of these reasons, Consumers Union thinks that most investors should steer clear of commodities trading.

An **option** is a contract giving the owner of an option the right to buy or sell an agreed-upon number of shares of a particular security (usually a common stock of a company) at a fixed price within a certain time period. Besides stock, options can be written on stock indices. There are two types of options: **puts** and **calls.** A put allows the option holder to sell the shares at a given price to a buyer who agrees in advance to take them. A call is the opposite transaction. It allows the holder to buy the securities at the agreed price, even if the market price at the time has gone higher.

Many exchanges allow options trading, and there is one specialized options exchange, the Chicago Board Options Exchange (CBOE). Most full-service brokerage firms and some specialized brokerages trade options.

Like commodities, the options market is highly complex and risky. The chief risk of buying an option is that the option will expire valueless, causing you to lose the entire sum you invested. Short trading of naked options can cause you to lose more than you invested. Like commodity futures, options trading requires you to predict not only *what* the market will do, but *when* it will do it (and it had better be soon!). A registered rep who is less than totally honest may try to convince you to trade options, because even though individual commissions may be small, options are repetitive transactions (they exist for a maximum of nine months). Thus, there will be more trades made and more commission income for the broker.

Options trading is best left to professionals who understand all the complexities associated with it and can properly judge the risks involved. Very few registered representatives really understand options well.

Foreign securities. Domestic investors can invest in some foreign companies via securities known as American Depository Receipts (ADRs). There are also a number of international mutual funds as well as investments in foreign currencies. With all the complexities of exchange rates, different monetary schemes, a changing political climate, and the like, this is a complicated and difficult area that takes years of experience to master. Some brokerage firms have a few foreign securities specialists, but do not expect the average broker to be especially knowledgeable in this area.

On the positive side, however, ADRs expand an investor's reach, allowing the purchase of shares in some outstanding companies outside the United States. In some cases, these securities may also be attractively priced. People who don't want to deal with the complexities of ADRs can get some of these advantages by buying shares in a mutual fund that invests abroad.

Other Products

There are dozens of other investment products. You can buy or sell a **real estate investment trust** (REIT), a **collateralized mortgage obligation** (CMO), a **zero-coupon bond,** or products with exotic names such as TIGRs. Some registered reps are licensed to sell life insurance and annuities in addition to securities. It is rare for a stockbroker to be as knowledgeable about insurance as he or she is about securities. If you need life insurance, check with a good insurance agent, who will conduct a needs analysis for you. You may find that the price offered by your broker is competitive with policies available from an insurance agent, but don't buy life insurance or an annuity from a registered rep without talking first with an insurance specialist. If you do buy insurance from a stockbroker, be sure that the premiums cannot be deducted from your **margin account** (see Glossary).

What's in a Name?

You can't always tell what you are purchasing by its name. A bond mutual fund that is called a "high-yield" fund probably is a risky junk-bond fund. A limited partnership may be called a "direct participation" security. Often this is done deliberately so you won't know what you are buying. It is necessary, therefore, to look beyond the name of a product to ascertain exactly what the investment is. Ask questions and read as much as you can about the investment. Brokers who are trying to sell you a product may not be totally forthcoming, so you have to do some work on your own to identify the product for what it is. Read the prospectus, as well as some combination of *The Value Line Investment Survey,* Standard & Poor's *Outlook* or *Stock Guide, The Wall Street Journal, Forbes, Fortune, Business Week,* and/ or *Barron's.* Use indexes or data bases to find information on the particular company or investment.

If you are not sure what a broker is offering, ask three pivotal questions:

• What kind of security is this?
• How does it work?
• What kind of commission will I be paying for it?

Information About Your Investments

Part of the broker's job is to give you information, good or bad, about your investments, especially if that information is not available in newspapers or other accessible sources of data. It is your job, too, to keep up with how your investments are doing.

Check the securities quotes in the newspaper. You can also subscribe to investment magazines and newsletters. Hundreds of books and periodicals are published every year concerning investing.

When you buy a security, note where the security is traded. If it is a stock or a bond, it could be traded on the New York Stock Exchange, the American Stock Exchange, one of the regional exchanges, or on the over-the-counter market. Once you know where the security is traded, you know where to look for the latest quote. The over-the-counter market utilizes a system known as **NASDAQ** (see Glossary) for reporting quotes. Some securities, particularly **penny stocks**, may trade only occasionally and may not be reported on the NASDAQ. They will probably be in what are known as the "pink sheets," which contain the latest trades for hard-to-find issues. (The sheets are, in fact, pink—hence the name.)

Mutual funds are among the most popular investments in America, so it is easy to find out how these funds are performing. The most efficient way to track performance is by utilizing a concept known as **net asset value** (NAV).

The fund will calculate (normally every business day) the value of all the securities in its portfolio. If the net asset value is on a downward trend, then the fund is not doing well. If the NAV trend is up, then the fund has performed well.

Finding performance information about limited partnerships that are not publicly traded is almost impossible. The only way a partner can obtain any data is by checking with the general partner, who may not always give an accurate picture of performance.

Keeping up with your investments can be time-consuming, but a qualified broker can assist you in obtaining information about your investments. Full-service firms are constantly generating research reports, projections, and other data for their clients.

Security Ratings

One way to determine the safety of a particular stock, bond, limited partnership, or mutual fund is by checking its ratings based on Value Line's opinion of how much that stock or group is likely to rise. Value Line, an independent rating firm, rates stocks and industry groups on a scale of 1 to 5, with 1 the highest. Value Line also provides historical and other useful data about different companies and their stock offerings. *The Value*

Line Investment Survey is published each week and is available at most public libraries.

Two other rating services, **Moody's Investors Service** and **Standard & Poor's,** rate corporate and municipal bonds based on the financial strength of the issuer. Moody's uses an initial capital letter followed by lowercase letters for its ratings—Aaa, for example, is the highest-rated bond. The next best rating is Aa, then A, Baa, and so forth. Standard & Poor's uses the same system, except it uses all capital letters. Its highest-rated bond is AAA, then AA, then A, and so on. Standard & Poor's *Stock Reports* and Moody's *Handbook of Common Stocks* are also available at most libraries.

Limited partnership offerings are also rated. Standard & Poor's rates them, as does the Robert A. Stanger organization. Numerical designations are used in both cases.

4 · THE FINANCIAL PROFESSIONALS

Not only are there hundreds of financial products to choose from, there also are a large number of financial professionals available. But choosing the wrong adviser can be hazardous to your wealth.

Stockbrokers

Stockbrokers earn that title by passing a series of examinations administered by the **National Association of Securities Dealers (NASD)**. Individual broker-dealers provide most broker training. That training by necessity concerns itself mainly with preparing aspiring brokers for the examinations they must pass to qualify as registered representatives. Depending on the broker-dealer, the potential brokers may also be trained in sales techniques and ethics. There is, in addition, a good deal of on-the-job training in telephone manners and sales strategies.

Registered reps need have no special expertise or training beyond what is required to pass the exams. Unless the broker-dealer demands it, there is no requirement for continuing education. As a result, it's possible that a registered rep may know very little about new financial instruments.

Remember that the primary function of a brokerage house is to induce the greatest number of customers to buy or sell securities. The most successful are not necessarily the most knowledgeable; rather, they are the best salespeople.

Investment Advisers

The financial professionals who are supposed to be experts at choosing securities and fitting them into a particular investor's portfolio usually are referred to as **investment advisers.** Brokers, ordinarily, advise people what to buy or sell, but they don't make the final decision. Investment advisers, also called money managers, often have discretion to buy and sell on the client's behalf without consulting the client on each transaction.

Investment advisers can work either for broker-dealers or as independent businesspeople. If they work for a broker-dealer, you may have to pay an extra fee on top of the regular brokerage commission.

Independent investment advisers usually charge a fee based on the total net worth of your portfolio. Some charge an extra increment if they are successful in making your portfolio grow by a certain amount.

An independent investment adviser works in one of two ways: (1) He or she draws up an investment plan for you to implement using your own registered rep, or (2) the adviser has a working relationship with a broker-dealer and will execute trades on your behalf. (This may entail an extra fee.) Or all the services may be packaged for one "wrap" fee, often as much as 3 percent of the assets managed per year.

Investment advisers, whether they work for a broker-dealer or independently, usually restrict their clientele to those who have a high net worth—say, $250,000—or a portfolio of a specified value, such as $100,000.

Some investment advisers have earned the right to carry the initials CFA (**chartered financial analyst**) after their names. This designation shows that they have passed an examination and have had continuing education in the area of financial analysis.

Since investment advisers make their living giving investment advice, *they must be registered with the SEC in that capacity.* (One exception: Advisers need not register if they are running a private investment partnership for 100 or fewer sophisticated investors.) Ask to see the registration, and never deal with an investment adviser who is not registered.

Financial Planners

There are few professions that grew faster during the 1980s than that of financial planner—a person who helps you chart your financial future. Financial planners do this primarily by preparing elaborate financial plans, giving investment advice, and selling financial products such as insurance or mutual funds.

Anybody can call himself or herself a financial planner, and it is not uncommon for insurance agents, stockbrokers, or investment advisers to call themselves financial planners in the hope of attracting more clients. At this writing, there are no federal regulatory or licensing standards for financial planners and few state regulations, although some states have legislation pending. Since there are no official standards, it is easy for a financial planner to perform unethical or illegal acts without anyone looking over his or her shoulder. Many financial planners work for themselves, and therefore are unsupervised. According to the National Association of Personal Financial Advisors (NAPFA), "the backgrounds of financial planners can vary as much as the services offered. The planner's education and background should demonstrate a solid foundation in financial planning and a commitment to keeping current."

There are, however, approximately 60,000 **certified financial planners** (CFPs) and they constitute the core of the legitimate profession. CFPs fall into four categories, depending on how they are compensated.

The largest group is known as *commission-only financial planners*. They get paid by recommending financial products to you, for which they earn a commission. Commissions are their *only* means of compensation. If, for example, they are licensed securities brokers, they may have an affiliation with a broker-dealer and will earn a commission on securities sales. Others may sell insurance, annuities, or similar products. But no matter what product they sell, these individuals have a built-in conflict of interest. They are likely to recommend only those products for which they are paid a commission, and they may do so even if the products are not suitable or appropriate for you.

It is not unusual for commission-only financial planners to try to attract clients by advertising themselves as "no-fee" financial advisers. While that statement is technically accurate, it is inaccurate from your point of view because it does not divulge the facts about how the planner is compensated. *One of your rights is to know how any financial adviser you choose is compensated.*

A second large group of planners is called *fee and commission planners*. They charge a fee (usually based on an hourly rate) for preparing a financial plan, in addition to earning commissions on products they sell. The fee is supposed to reduce the conflict-of-interest problem, but clients of such planners should still be prepared to ask tough questions about any products their planner tries to sell them.

Another group is known as *fee-offset planners*. You are charged a flat fee, against which any commissions earned by the planner are offset. An honest fee-offset planner credits to you any amount by which commissions earned exceed the fee.

Finally, there is a small group of practitioners who are *fee-only planners*. They sell no products, only their expertise, and they normally work only with high-net-worth clients. Their fees can range from $100 an hour and upward. Some charge a set hourly rate; others charge a flat fee or a fee based on a certain

range or within a set percentage of the value of your portfolio.

When dealing with a fee-only planner, ask if there is a cap on
fees charged.

NAPFA suggests that before you hire a financial planner, you
obtain specific and detailed answers to the following questions:

- What is your educational background and are you a CFP
(certified financial planner) or a ChFC (chartered financial
consultant)?
- How long have you been offering financial planning
services?
- What continuing education in financial planning do you
pursue on an annual basis?
- Are you a member of any of the major professional
financial planning associations—specifically, the Institute
of Financial Planners, the National Association of Personal
Financial Advisors (NAPFA), the International Association for
Financial Planning (IAFP), or the Registry of Financial
Planning Practitioners?
- Will you provide me with references from clients?
- Have you ever been cited by a professional or regulatory
governing body for disciplinary reasons?

Other Financial Professionals

There are a variety of other professionals who specialize in different aspects of financial planning, such as estates, insurance,
and taxes. Some of them may be registered reps and may, from
time to time, trade securities on behalf of others. No matter what
their specialty, however, if they are registered reps, they are
subject to the same rules and regulations (and hence the same
punishments) as those who make their primary living trading
for clients. Some planners are registered investment advisers,
which puts their actions under the jurisdiction of the SEC.

Before you do business with any financial professional, there are four things you *must* do:

1. Find out how he or she will be compensated. If the person is getting a commission from third parties, how much unbiased advice will you be getting?
2. Whatever you and the professional agree to, be sure to get—and keep—a written contract.
3. Determine how any disputes between the two of you will be resolved and be sure that is put into the contract.
4. Confirm your investment goals and risk tolerance in writing.

If the professional is not willing to put your agreement in writing or refuses to agree on how any disputes are to be settled, find someone else.

Credentials

There is a record of any financial professional's qualifications, and you can examine it. The trick is in knowing where to look.

All registered reps *must* be members of the NASD. A record of complaints against any rep is maintained there. Before doing business with any registered rep, obtain a copy of that record from NASD, Public Disclosure Program, P.O. Box 9401, Gaithersburg, Maryland 20898-9401.

What follows is a list of credentials and the organizations that grant them. If a person claims to have a given designation, there should be a record, although you may have to look elsewhere for a record of complaints.

- Attorney-at-Law: the local or state bar association of the state in which he or she practices
- Certified Financial Planner (CFP): College for Financial Planning, 9725 E. Hampden Avenue, Denver, Colorado 80231

- Certified Public Accountant: the local organization of CPAs
- Chartered Financial Analyst (CFA): Institute of Chartered Financial Analysts, P.O. Box 3668, Charlottesville, Virginia 22903
- Chartered Life Underwriter (CLU) and Chartered Financial Consultant (ChFC): The American College, 270 Bryn Mawr Avenue, Bryn Mawr, Pennsylvania 19010-9989
- Associated Person (commodity broker): National Futures Association, 120 Broadway, New York, New York 10271

To keep their credentials up-to-date, many practitioners must attend continuing-education programs annually. When you check with these professional organizations, inquire whether the individual has maintained the designation status with continuing-education credits.

Investor Realities

If you are a small investor who invests only occasionally, you may not receive the same attention from a broker or financial planner as someone who generates a lot of commission income. However, there are a substantial number of planners and registered reps who have made a very good living working with the smaller investor. Your best bet for finding such a person is to ask other small investors for recommendations. Then thoroughly investigate him or her.

There is no minimum that you must invest. As long as you meet the general suitability guidelines of the broker-dealer with whom you are doing business, you can invest. However, you shouldn't invest unless you can meet your regular bills every month, have your debts under control, have adequate insurance, and have an adequate savings cushion in a bank or money market account. Once you have taken care of those matters and you have some extra funds you'd like to put to work, investing becomes the next step toward financial security.

5 · IN BROKERS WE TRUST

People often seek the advice of experts: When they are sick, they visit a physician; if they have legal questions, they consult a lawyer. Because they know little or nothing about medicine or law, they must place their trust and faith in professionals. The identical circumstances apply to investing.

People seek investment advice from experts and trust them with a very precious commodity, their money. They expect these experts to help them stay ahead of inflation while at the same time achieving their financial objectives. However, just as there are some doctors and lawyers who are incompetent or even unscrupulous, there are financial professionals who violate the trust placed in them.

This concept of trust in financial matters is so important that the law gives a special status to anyone who handles other people's money. They are known as **fiduciaries**. Bankers are fiduciaries. So are attorneys and, of course, stockbrokers. A fiduciary has an affirmative duty *always* to act in a positive manner toward his principal—the client. He or she must exhibit a selfless devotion toward the well-being of the customer's money and refrain from any conduct that would harm the investment. It is this status as a fiduciary that more than anything else defines how a broker is supposed to act toward a customer.

Any individual who violates his or her duty as a fiduciary has broken the law. The law spells out what options are available to those who have suffered as a result of such a violation. Investment laws and regulations were put into place to make sure that the system will be fair.

Who Are the Brokers?

For the most part, if you want to acquire an investment product, you have to seek out a person who sells these products. These salespeople had to pass a series of tests that qualified them to sell those products, and they are subject to regulation by the government and their own industry. However, just because this professional has demonstrated some expertise in financial products, it does not always follow that he or she is competent to render financial advice. His or her primary role remains that of a salesperson.

You need to keep in mind that a conflict of interest exists. A broker makes his or her living selling the very products that you are asking him or her to evaluate. The financial advice you receive may therefore be biased. For example, if you seek advice from a broker on two different products, the broker might recommend the one that gives him or her the higher commission, not the one that is most suitable for you.

Financial professionals who sell investment products are given a variety of titles by the companies for which they work, but all of these titles are designed primarily to disguise the fact that they are salespeople. Although officially called registered representatives, they may be referred to as brokers, account executives, financial counselors, financial executives, investment consultants, or some other fancy title. If, however, you always think of them as salespeople whose job it is to get you to buy something, then you will be less likely to act foolishly.

The conduct of these salespeople is supervised by their employers, federal and state regulatory authorities, and stock exchanges, but frequently that supervision is severely lacking, especially at the lowest level. Often it is the investor who is in the best position to spot any unlawful conduct. You should remain on your guard at all times.

Training and Sales Techniques

When a broker first enters the securities business, he or she will be trained by the broker-dealer who has done the hiring. Training usually involves a combination of product knowledge and sales techniques. Brokers are also schooled in the legalities and details of customer accounts, recordkeeping, and ethics. Some broker-dealers do a better training job than others. The training period may last as long as four to six months, after which most firms have their trainees start soliciting customers by phone.

One of the most common sales solicitation techniques is the "cold call," in which the fledgling salesperson telephones customers from a list or from the telephone book. The salesperson and the potential customer have never met, and the salesperson may not know whether the individual he or she is calling is an investor or is even interested in investing.

Potential investors are also reached in other ways. The marketing departments of broker-dealers produce glossy brochures promoting products that the firms are selling. However, these brochures may make exaggerated claims or, more important, omit some vital piece of information. Put no more credence in these brochures and pamphlets than you do in any other form of advertising.

Do not be deceived by ads run by securities firms to solicit new business. A newspaper or magazine advertisement may, for instance, discuss the high returns of a specific bond but omit (or note only in very small type) the fact that the bond is callable. Or an ad for a mutual fund may not mention that there is a back-end load when the fund is sold. Although there may not be a specific violation of laws or regulations here, you nevertheless can be misled. Approach an ad for a financial product or purveyor with a healthy dose of skepticism.

Incentives

The brokerage business is a sales business in which **incentives** are common. Registered representatives make their living by inducing people to buy or sell securities. The more business the registered rep does, the more profit he or she creates for the rep and his or her firm. To keep their reps enthusiastic, brokerage houses often run contests or offer prizes to their highest salespeople. The incentive might be a ski trip to Switzerland or two weeks in Hawaii. Second- and third-place winners might receive a watch or box seats at the local ballpark.

In order to expedite the contest, the broker-dealer may have a "stock of the day" that they ask their reps to push. You might receive a phone call from your broker urging you to buy a stock that does not fit your investor profile. During these contest periods, brokers have a tendency to get excited and forget about your needs.

Registered reps are evaluated by their employers primarily on one criterion—how much of the product they can sell every day. Those brokers who are the big producers will be retained; those who don't produce could lose their jobs. Thus, registered reps are under a good deal of pressure.

Proprietary Products

Many of the larger full-service broker-dealers offer their own money market funds, mutual funds, unit investment trusts, or limited partnerships. These in-house products are called **proprietary**. As the sponsor of the products, the broker-dealer stands to gain substantial profits from their sale. Broker-dealers also earn continuing management fees on an annual basis on these proprietary products. Therefore, the broker-dealer often offers its registered reps incentives—perhaps a higher-than-usual commission—to sell the product.

These products can be very safe or very risky, but because a potential conflict of interest exists, be wary of any registered rep who wants to sell you only proprietary products. If you constantly receive recommendations for proprietary products, ask to see performance information and data on competing products so that you can make a decision on your own. Make sure you don't make your investment choices from an artificially narrow menu.

Investment Banking

Besides executing trades for investors, many large broker-dealers are also in the investment banking business. Investment banking involves advising companies on how to issue stocks or bonds, and then underwriting the stock or bond issues. The **underwriter** buys a large portion of a stock or bond offering from a company at a set price and then sells that offering to the public, usually at a markup. For example, a broker-dealer might buy out the entire stock offering—1 million shares—of New Company. The broker-dealer pays $2 million, or $2 a share. New Company gets its $2 million immediately and is now able to invest that money in its company. Meanwhile, the broker-dealer has 1 million shares of stock that it must sell. Say the broker-dealer puts a price of $2.25 on the stock. If it can sell all the shares for that amount, it will have a profit of $250,000. This, of course, is extremely lucrative for the firm, and it is another instance where incentives are common.

Don't get caught in your broker's excitement. If he or she temporarily forgets your rights, you must remember them. Don't hesitate to rein in your broker when appropriate.

Recommendations from the House

Most of the larger broker-dealers have research departments whose function is to evaluate and recommend specific securities. Research departments usually produce a report concluding that a given security should be bought, held, or sold. Registered reps often use these reports to generate new business. If a broker-dealer issues a research report on General Motors, for example, recommending that it be purchased at the current price because it appears that the price will rise soon, a registered rep will suggest that you buy shares of General Motors based on the report.

Research reports frequently come with suitability recommendations, such as, "This stock is recommended for conservative portfolios" or "This stock is suitable for those who are interested in growth." If you are asked to invest in a recommended security, be sure that it meets *your* needs. Ask for a copy of the recommendation and read it thoroughly before you invest. Don't buy or sell anything on the basis of a research report until you have examined the report yourself. Also, don't assume that just because the research report is produced by "experts," it is correct. Even experts make mistakes.

Research departments are not profit centers for broker-dealers: They produce no income. Therefore, to justify the expense of carrying such a department, there have to be enough sales.

Registered Representatives Changing Firms

Changing firms is a way of life for many brokers. Moreover, often one firm merges with another firm that has an entirely different system and set of procedures. When a change occurs, the registered rep is expected to bring his or her "book of business"—that is, clients—to the new firm.

You may have to decide whether to go with your old broker or to search out a new one. If your broker has moved or been merged with another firm, and you decide to stay with that broker, it is vital to understand that the paperwork you did when you opened the account with the old firm may *not* be applicable to the new one. This change gives you an opportunity to reassess your suitability requirements and your investment goals. You will need to do new paperwork and establish a new relationship with the branch manager.

At the new firm, your broker probably will be under some pressure to make a good initial impression. Let's say that the new firm is a co–general partner on a new limited-partnership offering. In this situation, your old broker may urge you to buy into the partnership, regardless of its suitability for your portfolio.

Be cautious if you follow a broker to a new employer. If procedures are different there, demand an explanation and be sure you are satisfied with the answer.

Choosing a Registered Representative You Can Trust

Choosing a broker need not be a hit-or-miss proposition. You want someone who understands your particular investment philosophy and someone with whom you feel comfortable.

Check on the broker's disciplinary history. Obtain from the NASD an Information Request Form that will allow you to find out about any serious violations committed by the broker (call 301-590-6500).

Once you have narrowed your search, ask the potential broker the following questions:

• Will he or she act as a financial adviser and recommend certain securities and courses of action? You may or may not want a broker who is simply an order taker.

• What is his or her attitude toward highly speculative investments? If you are conservative, you don't want a broker who is constantly recommending risky investments.

- What is his or her standard operating procedure with customers? For example, does the broker meet with customers regularly to review their portfolios? Does he or she take calls during certain hours?
- Will you always be fully and promptly informed of all actions taken on your behalf?
- Who will handle your account if the broker is ill or on vacation? Ask to meet that person.

Listen not only to the answers but also to how they are presented. Responses such as, "Don't worry about it" or "We'll cross that bridge when we come to it" should disqualify any potential candidate. You want specifics and details. Choose the candidate who makes the best presentation *and* seems to understand most closely your investment philosophy, needs, and wants. A broker–client relationship is very personal, and you are not stuck with it forever. Always remember that the broker is working for you and on your behalf. If the broker at any time fails to meet your standards, it is time to look for a new one.

6 · OPENING AN ACCOUNT

Once you have chosen a broker, your work is only half finished. The registered rep works for a broker-dealer, and if the broker-dealer doesn't do a good job, the best rep in the world will be helpless to give you good service.

After choosing the broker, ask to meet his or her manager. Ask the manager about the firm's procedures for handling customer complaints. By doing that, you are telling the broker and the manager that you are planning to keep a sharp eye on your account and will be prepared to make a complaint if one is warranted. As mentioned previously, also ask to meet whoever will take over your account if your broker is sick or on vacation.

Account Types

The majority of individual investors opt for a **cash account**, which means all securities purchased are paid for in cash (for this purpose, a check is considered cash). You must pay no later than the **settlement date**, normally five business days after the trade has been made. The bill you receive includes the cost of the securities plus the broker's commission.

If you sell securities, you will be paid the proceeds—less broker commission—a few days after settlement.

You can open a money market account with the broker-dealer and instruct your broker to deposit proceeds into or deduct funds from your account. In either case, with a cash account, all transactions are settled entirely in cash.

Margin Accounts

Margin accounts are credit accounts, and they are a riskier way of doing business. A margin account allows you to use **leverage**, or borrowing power, when purchasing securities. As a result, you can buy more securities for a given amount of money. This increases the size of any profit, but it also increases the size of any potential loss. Consumers Union believes most people would be wiser not to buy on margin.

Here's how a margin account works. Assume, for example, that you want to buy 100 shares of IBM, which is selling at $100 a share. If you had a cash account, you would have to send the broker-dealer a check for $10,000 (or it would have to be taken out of your account) within five days of settlement. With a margin account, you can buy the same 100 shares for $5,000 (assuming 50 percent margin, the usual amount these days).

How come? Because you borrow the balance of $5,000 from the brokerage firm. You don't ordinarily repay this $5,000 loan until you sell the stock. The 100 shares of IBM are put into your margin account and they stand as collateral for the loan.

To open a margin account, you are required to make an initial cash contribution, usually $2,000. At any point, you can increase your borrowing power by adding to the account more cash or securities you already own that are "marginable." (Most securities except penny stocks and some limited partnership units are marginable.) The larger the value of the cash and securities in your account, the more borrowing power you have.

By law, the amount of credit a broker-dealer can give to its margin-account clients is limited. At present, the amount is 50 percent of the initial purchase price, but it could be raised or lowered by the Federal Reserve Board, which is responsible for this process.

The brokerage house, of course, is not going to lend you that $5,000 without charging interest. There is no set interest rate on margin accounts, but it usually is a bit above the prime rate. When you open the margin account, the firm must, under the federal Truth in Lending Law, tell you their current interest rate and the circumstances under which it will fluctuate. Under the law, you must also be informed when there is a change in the rate.

Returning to our example: You purchased $10,000 worth of stock for $5,000. You don't have to put out any more money until you sell the stock *or* until the value of the stock falls below a percentage set by the Federal Reserve, the stock exchange, or your brokerage firm. If there is a drop in stock market prices and your equity falls below the minimum, you will be subjected to a **margin call**, which requires you to add cash or marginable securities to the account. Margin calls always seem to occur at the worst possible moment, and they may force you to sell a stock when you don't want to do so. (Indeed, they may force you to sell a stock that otherwise could have been held profitably for a long-term recovery.) If sufficient cash is not brought in on a margin call, your stocks will be liquidated automatically, at a loss to you. Even after the stock is sold, you may still owe your broker-dealer a balance on the funds you borrowed to make the original stock purchase.

Broker-dealers make a good deal of money on the interest they earn on margin accounts, and many registered reps encourage the use of margin by as many clients as possible. But the interest you pay also cuts your potential profits or widens your losses—another reason why CU thinks most people should not mess around with margin.

Since the margin account is vastly different from a cash account, firms may require customers who wish to trade on margin to sign a margin agreement. Margin agreements typically detail the rules and regulations governing the account, the amount of equity required, and the interest rate to be charged.

Cash Management Accounts

You can find yourself agreeing to a margin account without even being aware of it. This occurs in the case of certain **cash management accounts** that provide checking and credit card privileges. The fine print in these agreements often includes your consent to use margin under certain circumstances.

Cash management accounts can be convenient, but any investor who wants to open one should inquire whether the account agreement includes a consent to margin buys. If it does, you might want to give the account a second thought because of the risks associated with margin and margin accounts.

Jeff and Gina Jackson didn't inquire about margin accounts, nor did they even know what margin was when they opened their cash management account at a large brokerage house. They decided to open the account when Gina inherited $30,000 from an aunt who died a few months earlier. Jeff and Gina were investing novices, but a former schoolmate of Jeff's advised them to open a cash management account. The broker who opened the account for the Jacksons failed to mention margin or the fact that they were, in effect, opening a margin account when they signed up for the cash management account.

The Jacksons made a number of purchases of stock on their broker's recommendation and paid for the stock through their cash management account. When the stock market took a tumble and stayed down, the Jacksons soon found that they had to respond to a margin call. When they couldn't, most of their account was liquidated. Jeff and Gina lost $22,000.

The cash management account is a hybrid. Many brokerage firms offer it under a variety of names. To open one, you deposit a minimum amount in cash and/or securities. It operates very much like a margin account, since it frequently provides check-writing with overdraft privileges and credit cards. The securities in the account act as collateral for any overdrafts or credit card balances, so margin regulations must be followed.

Trades may be settled with either cash or credit using margin. Often there is a checking feature that allows you to write a check for any purpose, with the money being deducted from the cash management account. However, the minimum balance must be maintained. Some cash management accounts have an additional feature: Any unused portion is invested in the money market, earning interest on the balance.

Since cash management accounts permit margin trading, all of the rules governing margin accounts apply to these accounts as well. On October 19, 1987, many investors who had only cash management accounts were forced to meet margin calls because the value of their securities slipped below the required limits. But remember that margin calls need not be triggered by a market crash; they occur much more frequently than that. Nevertheless, cash management accounts are popular. Some people even use them instead of a bank checking account.

Custodial Accounts

All brokerage firms accept **custodial accounts**—accounts established by an adult for a minor. The adult usually is the contributor to the account and the funds are held on the minor's behalf. Such accounts traditionally are used as savings vehicles for college. Assets in the account belong to the minor, so if you set up a custodial account for your child, you cannot withdraw the funds to buy a house. The rules governing custodial accounts are explained in the Uniform Gift to Minors Act. Custodial accounts should employ very conservative investment philosophies. It goes without saying that brokers should handle such accounts with kid gloves.

Managed Accounts

In a **managed account,** you give up all decision-making power over which stocks to buy and sell to a broker. Not only does the broker decide what securities to buy and sell, he or she also decides when to buy and sell.

Instead of paying a commission on every trade, you are charged an annual flat fee based on the value of the account. If the value of the account rises or falls, the fee rises or falls as well; the percentage stays the same. Thus, it is in the manager's interest to increase the value of the account, rather than simply to make a lot of transactions to earn more commissions.

Managed accounts handled by experienced, knowledgeable individuals are suitable for investors who don't have the time or knowledge to manage their own investments.

Other Accounts

You can have more than one kind of account with a single brokerage firm. Just as you might have both savings and checking accounts at your local bank, you might have a cash account, a money market account, and an IRA with one brokerage house. If you want to trade commodities, you will be required to open a separate account.

Selling Short

Selling short requires that you have a margin account. This strategy is used when you think that the price of an individual stock or a group of stocks will fall. You borrow (not buy) the stock from the brokerage house and sell the stock to someone who thinks the price of the stock will go up. For example, if you think that the stock of Ford, which is selling at $60 a share, will fall, you can instruct your broker to sell 100 shares of Ford short. Since you don't own any shares of Ford, the firm will lend you, say, 100 shares that are selling at $60. If you are right and the stock falls to $55, you can then buy your borrowed shares at $55. Since you have already sold them at $60, you have made $5 a share, or $500. Selling short is a high-risk investment strategy used by highly sophisticated investors and investment specialists; it is not recommended for most investors. For one thing, the stock market has a long-term historical tendency to rise. It's no cinch even to make money swimming *with* the tide; swimming *against* it is harder.

Even more important, the potential loss on a short sale is unlimited, while the maximum potential gain is generally considered to be 100 percent. (Calculating the gain on a short sale is mathematically tricky, for reasons we won't go into here.) This is the reverse of normal investing, where potential gains are unlimited and the maximum possible loss is 100 percent.

Orders

As a fiduciary and agent, your broker must follow your directions. When you want to buy or sell a security, the broker is given an "order" to execute. Although it is wise to seek your broker's advice before making a final determination, it is up to you to decide the type of order.

If you trade stocks, it is important to understand that the stock market is an **auction market.** That is, prices are determined on a bid-and-ask basis. The broker for a seller will determine, based on the last sale made, how much to ask for a specific security. The broker for a buyer will determine, on the same basis, how much to offer. The deal usually is struck somewhere in between. Prices are normally quoted in eighths of a dollar, or 12½ cents. For example, in a rising market, if the last trade on IBM common stock was $100 a share, the seller's broker might ask for $100.25. The buyer's broker, who is required to get the best price for his or her client, might come back with an offer of $100 and 12½ cents (called 100 and 1/8). If the seller's broker agrees to that price, the trade is made. Remember that the seller's broker is obligated to sell the shares at the best price obtainable, but ordinarily the shares *must* be sold. So if the best price is 100 and 1/8, he or she will take it rather than wait a long time for a higher price.

A client who is trading on the stock market probably will give one of two types of orders to his or her broker:

1. The **market order.** The overwhelming majority of all trades are market orders. The market order instructs the broker to buy or sell a security at the prevailing market price. Speed of execution is as important as price.

2. **Open, or good-till-canceled, orders.** Open orders may have a time limit attached to them. These orders instruct the broker to buy or sell a stock at a price that has yet to be reached. The order remains open until it is canceled by the customer or the deadline expires. For example, you might want to buy a stock, but not at its present price of $10 a share. You can tell your broker that if and when the stock falls to $6 a share, you want to buy 100 shares. Your broker will enter your order and keep track of the stock. The stock could reach $6 tomorrow, next week, next month, or never. Your order to buy it at $6 remains open until you cancel it, or the deadline expires, or until the stock drops to $6 and the trade is executed automatically. Similarly, you can tell your broker to sell a stock you bought at $10 whenever it reaches $15.

The **stop loss order** is a form of open order. Sometimes the price of a security can drop quickly. Unless you act equally fast, you might miss the opportunity to sell your shares at a profit. Say you purchased a stock at $15 a share, it is now trading at $30, but you think it might start falling. You can instruct your broker to put a stop loss, to sell the stock if and when it hits $25. If the stock does fall quickly and hits $25, you still will have made $10 a share profit, whereas if you had waited and put in your sell order as the stock was falling, it might have fallen to $23 or even less before your order was executed. When your stock reaches the selling point you have designated—$25, in this example—it becomes a market order and the trade is consummated at the next price, which may be more or less than $25 a share but usually is pretty close. You have saved part of your profit.

Unfortunately, stop loss orders don't work well under chaotic market conditions, such as the crash of 1987. In a plummeting market, your order might be triggered when the stock falls below $25, but the very next stop might be, say, $22.

There are many other types of orders. Ask your broker to explain them and consider whether any meet your specific needs.

Orders help you preserve your capital, stem losses, and lock in profits. They should not be used willy-nilly; they should be part of a well-thought-out investment strategy. It is vital that you fully understand the purpose of each order and the way it fits into your overall portfolio strategy. A well-schooled and interested broker should be able to explain clearly and easily what each order is intended to do.

7 · RULES AND PROCEDURES

The investment system is set up to foster fairness. The small individual investor is supposed to be treated as fairly as larger clients with more financial clout. Most brokers meet the strict standards, but every once in a while, the system breaks down. Abuses do occur.

Registered representatives play a role similar to that of a trustee—that is, they must be honest and trustworthy. Their only thoughts should be of their clients' interest. Even though most stockbrokers are honest and capable, you need to know how to protect yourself.

The securities laws include rules that registered reps and broker-dealers must follow to protect clients. Reps or broker-dealers should not react passively or stand by and watch a problem develop. They must engage in what is legally called "an affirmative duty" to act.

A failure to act when one should have acted can itself constitute a securities violation. For example, if you are determined to invest in a highly risky enterprise, and that risk is inappropriate considering your circumstances or investment needs, your broker has an affirmative duty to discourage you. He or she is not allowed to sit there and allow it to happen without warning you of the consequences. If you go ahead and make the investment after the warning, the broker has done his or her duty. But the warning must be given.

Ultimately, you are responsible for your actions, but your registered rep must act as a fiduciary—that is, give only advice that will advance your goals. The law does not expect that the advice given will always be right, or even that it will always be taken, but it does insist that a good-faith effort be made to deliver the best advice possible.

The securities laws are meant to prevent fraudulent actions by registered reps and broker-dealers. However, the fraudulent act must be intentional, not accidental. What follows are examples of intentional acts that have been found to be fraudulent and hence violations of the securities laws.

New-Account Forms

Dishonesty may begin right at the start of the broker–client relationship. Every investment firm requires that the broker speak with you and fill out a **new-account form**. The broker must interview you to get all the necessary information. All lines and blanks on the form must be filled in. *This form becomes the basis of all future recommendations made to you after the account is opened.*

During the interview, the broker must determine your income, net worth (what you own minus what you owe), and, most important, investment philosophy. An honest broker records your actual responses to the questions. Let's assume the answers are $50,000 in income, $100,000 in net worth, and a low-risk strategy or goal such as "income with preservation of capital."

However, a broker could fill in different answers, such as $100,000 for income, $500,000 for net worth, and "high-risk" for the investment philosophy. By doing this, he or she could later justify to his or her superiors the high-risk recommendations he or she made to you.

That's what happened to Karen Lee. When Karen turned twenty-one a few years ago, her grandmother gave her an old but beautiful necklace that had been in the family for years. Karen's grandmother had said the necklace was valuable, but since it was known that the grandmother tended to exaggerate, nobody took the older woman seriously. As it turned out, the necklace was *very* valuable. When Karen had it appraised, she was overwhelmed to discover that it was worth $60,000. Karen sold the necklace for its value and then wanted to invest the $60,000 windfall. She was about to be married, so she was hoping she and her future husband could use the money toward the purchase of a house.

Because she knew little about investing, however, she was interested when she received a general mail solicitation from a broker. Karen proceeded to open an account with the broker, and when the broker asked Karen to sign the various papers necessary to open the account, Karen asked what she was signing. The broker replied, "It's just a formality; everyone signs the same forms; don't worry about it." So Karen signed. Although she didn't know it at the time, she signed a consent to trade options and a margin agreement. It took less than a year for the broker to run the account to just under $9,000. Not much of a wedding present for Karen. Registered representatives can get away with this because investors normally never see their new-account form. It goes directly into the firm's file, and the information often goes right into a computer.

Protect yourself by asking for a copy of the form. Be sure that all the answers to your questions are properly recorded and that all lines and blanks are filled in correctly. In addition, write a letter to the broker, with a copy to his or her manager, repeating your answers to the interview questions—particularly the ones involving income, net worth, and investment philosophy. Both letters should be certified, with a return receipt requested. Be sure to keep a copy of the letter.

At the same time, start your own file. It should contain a correct copy of the new-account form as well as a copy of your confirming letter. Once you begin trading, put into the file all confirmations, statements, and other paperwork pertaining to your investment account and activities.

As an additional check, send an annual letter to your broker and his or her manager (preferably on the anniversary date of the opening of your account) reiterating the information regarding your income, net worth, and investment philosophy. If any of that information becomes outdated, update it in a new letter and ask that a revised account form be filled out and sent to you. Letting your broker know that you are keeping a file of all your investment communications can be a deterrent to dishonesty.

You will need to follow this same procedure for any account you open, whether it is a simple IRA or a commodities account. There is no substitute for well-documented information. An up-to-date and complete file on securities transactions will also make it easy to find the appropriate documents when you record your profits or losses for income taxes.

You will generally not be expected to sign the new-account form on opening an account. But others may be presented for signature, such as a margin-account form or a consent to trade options. *Don't sign any form without reading it thoroughly and don't sign any form with blank spaces on it.* Ask your broker to explain anything you don't understand. Never accept statements such as, "This is all standard; you don't need to read it" or "Nobody really reads those forms."

Suitability

Joan Chapman is a novice to the world of investing. When her husband, Eric, died suddenly, he left her $500,000 in insurance, part of which was to go toward educating Joan's two teenage daughters. Eric was an excellent provider who handled all investment and financial matters himself. Joan had no idea what to do with the insurance money that came to her in one lump sum.

On the advice of her brother, Joan visited and quickly selected a broker who seemed to be an expert on investing. Joan gave him $100,000 to invest for the girls' college. Since Joan was a neophyte investor and the money was to be used for education, Joan's portfolio should have reflected the most conservative investment philosophy. Instead, the broker wrote down that Joan was willing to take some risks. The broker proceeded to put Joan's money into high-risk options and penny stocks. It took only about six months for Joan to lose virtually all of her money.

Your registered representative is required to follow your investment philosophy. All securities have certain risk characteristics that fit into a similar risk tolerance for investors. A registered representative who recommends unsuitable securities has not acted as a fiduciary. If you are wronged, immediately take the actions specified in chapter 11.

Suitability and IRAs

Many Americans have established **Individual Retirement Accounts** (IRAs) with brokerage firms. Financial planners and other financial experts advise that IRAs should be treated differently from other investment accounts. Because IRAs are set up with the express purpose of providing a retirement nest egg, you should approach IRA investing with a bit more caution. Even if you are willing to take some risks with your regular investment account, think twice about taking the same risks with your IRA. Any registered rep who doesn't discuss this situation with you is not doing his or her job.

Affordability

A factor of suitability is **affordability**. A common mistake is to invest more than you can afford. A young person with a steady income can probably afford to invest more than a retired individual living on a fixed income. Your broker must be acutely aware of all your financial circumstances. One of the questions a broker should ask during your initial interview is how much you can set aside for investing. If you determine that the maximum is $10,000 a year, a broker who recommends that you put $15,000 into your portfolio violates the securities laws, as does the broker who exposes you to more risk than you can afford with certain margin, options, and commodities strategies. Your broker should also keep you from spending too much, whether on a speculative "hot tip" or a conservative investment. A broker who asks you whether you can really afford to lay out the money you propose is doing his or her job and is acting in a prudent, trustee-like manner.

Your suitability requirements, your investment philosophy, and data on how much you can afford (generally determined by your net worth and available cash) constitute your **investment profile**. A competent registered rep will have drawn up a thorough investment profile on you and will refer to it before making any recommendations or final investment decisions. Any deviation from the investment profile must have a good explanation or it can be considered a violation of securities laws.

Diversification

Another suitability-related problem is **diversification** or the lack of it. A registered rep who puts all of your investment funds into one security without taking into account your other holdings could be held liable, depending on the particular circumstances of the account.

It might be perfectly suitable, for example, for a broker to put all of your investment funds into government bonds if your goal is to have a retirement nest egg in five years. On the other hand, recommending penny stocks to you if you have no other investments is an unsuitable lack of diversification.

8 · SELF-DEFENSE

Before you invest in any security, be sure you can answer all the
questions in this self-protection checklist:

- What are my investment goals?
- What is my risk tolerance?
- Does this investment meet my investment goals? How do I know?
- Does it meet my suitability criteria? How do I know?
- Have I researched the investment?
- Do I know how it works and the risks associated with it? What is my potential maximum loss on this investment?
- Are there any limitations with regard to the investment? Am I aware of the implications of those limitations?
- Have I discussed this investment with at least one financial professional?
- Have I determined at what price I want to buy the investment?
- Have I thought about when and at what price I want to sell the investment?
- What is a realistic estimate of the potential profit from

this investment? How much of that potential profit would come from income (such as dividends or interest) and how much from capital gains?

• Do I know all the fees and expenses that I may have to pay and under what circumstances I will have to pay them?

• Who recommended the security to me? Have I explored the circumstances surrounding the recommendation?

• Are there any tax consequences associated with the purchase or sale of the investment? Do I fully understand them?

Keeping Accurate Records

Every time you place an order with your broker, whether in person or on the phone, record the date and time of the conversation and take notes.

The best defensive measure you can employ is to keep accurate records of all your investment transactions. Stationery stores sell securities recordkeeping books. If you own a home computer, there are software packages that will aid you in keeping records. For tax purposes, too, you have to have records of your profits or losses. Hold on to all investment paperwork just as you save all tax returns and records.

Note next to the record of the transaction two things— whether you gave the broker any kind of order, such as a stop loss, and whether the trade was your idea or your broker's. *Do this with every trade.* When you receive your confirmation slip, check to see whether it is marked "solicited" or "unsolicited." *Solicited* means the trade was the broker's idea, *unsolicited* means it was yours. If the confirmation slip does not match your records, complain immediately. The broker will have to produce similar notes and records in the event of a legal dispute. At the least, you will be able to see how effective your broker's advice has been.

Recommendation Follow-Up

If your broker recommends a particular security, don't buy it immediately. Request a detailed letter explaining why the recommendation is a good one and particularly why it is suitable for you. See if the letter matches the sales pitch. In any event, keep the letter with your other investment information.

Confirmations and Statements

After every trade, you will receive a **confirmation** slip from the brokerage house. Check it carefully against your written record. If there is a discrepancy, contact your broker immediately. Keep these confirmations. Every month you will also receive a **statement** showing the current state of your holdings and the activity in your account during that period. Again, check the statement and the confirmations against each other and against your records. Some brokerage firms also give you periodic written updates or summaries of your account activity, over and beyond the monthly statements they are required to send you.

Every six months, check over all confirmations and statements, comparing them with your own records. Look back and see whether all stop loss, limit, or other special orders you issued have in fact been carried out. If not, demand an explanation. All open orders—i.e., stop loss—must appear on confirmations and on statements. If they don't, that means they have not been placed—no matter what your broker tells you.

Reading a Statement

You should reconcile your brokerage statement each month in the same way that you reconcile your checking account. With your checking account, you compare your canceled checks with your banking statement. With a brokerage account, you compare your confirmations with the brokerage statement.

Although not all statements are identical, all contain the same basic information. The overall format shows monthly activity in one section and all holdings (your portfolio) in another.

1. Check the opening and closing balances. Be aware, however, that trades made near the end of the month may not appear—just like a bank, the broker-dealer has a statement closing date.

2. Make sure that all trades appear in the proper column. If you have only a cash account, nothing should show up in the margin-account column. Buys are sometimes followed by "DR," which means that amount will be deducted from (debited to) your account; a sell is followed by "CR," money now added (credited) to your account.

3. Check that all dividends and interest have been properly credited to your account. Note that stocks generate dividends, while bonds generate interest. Therefore, if your portfolio includes only stocks, there should be no notation of interest earned.

4. Portfolio values or totals, which usually appear at the bottom of the statement, should be correct.

5. In the "Summary of Value" section there may be columns marked "Long" and "Short." "Long" refers to all the securities you actually own (you have paid for them in full). "Short" refers to securities that have been borrowed and sold. If you have a cash account, there should be no notations in the "Short" column.

6. Some forms have a column headed "Estimated Annual Income—Rate/Amount." This is an estimate expressed both as a percentage and actual dollar amount of the expected income on your investment, calculated on the value of the security at the time the statement is issued.

7. If you have a margin account, you may find three headings and corresponding numbers under Portfolio Information:
Priced Portfolio Value
Net Worth
Available for Borrowing

The largest number, "Priced Portfolio Value," refers to the market value of the securities; "Net Worth" is the portfolio value in the account minus any sums borrowed from the broker-dealer to buy securities; the last number tells how much money is available for borrowing.

8. On some statements, under Transaction Description, you might find the notation "exchanged." This means the actual sale or purchase was recorded earlier but now the actual shares have been received or delivered.

Annual Broker Meeting

Schedule a face-to-face meeting with your broker at least once a year. Review your investment goals and be sure that you both are still in agreement about your investment needs. It is a good idea to have the broker's manager attend the meeting as well. Not only does that give you another opportunity to meet the manager, it also permits that individual to know you a little better. Of course, if there is a new manager since your last meeting with your broker, make an extra effort to have him or her meet with the two of you.

After the annual meeting, again write a letter to confirm what happened and specifically to reconfirm your financial goals, risk tolerance, and other objectives.

Reading a Prospectus

If you invest in an initial public offering, a public limited partnership, a mutual fund, or some other types of investments, you must be given a **prospectus**, a disclosure document required by the SEC. A prospectus is a lengthy, formidable-looking document that lays out the advantages and disadvantages of the investment.

At a minimum, read the following portions of the document and be sure you understand them:

1. Every prospectus has a section entitled "Who Should Invest?" or something similar. Here the suitability standards necessary to invest in this security are laid out in great detail. If you don't meet the standards, don't invest. You should also bring that fact to the attention of the individual who tried to sell you the investment.

For example, the suitability requirements for a public limited partnership may be as follows:

Interests will only be sold to an individual who makes a minimum purchase of 10 interests ($5,000) and represents in writing that he or she has either (1) a net worth (exclusive of home, home furnishings, and automobiles) of at least $30,000, plus an annual gross income of at least $30,000, or (2) a net worth (exclusive of home, home furnishings, and automobiles) of at least $75,000.

The suitability requirements are always defined in terms of the investor's net worth and gross income. Not everyone, for example, can meet the standards quoted above. If, for instance, you do not have an annual gross income of at least $30,000 or a total net worth exceeding $75,000, you are not eligible to buy into this partnership, and a broker or other financial professional who sells you this partnership has violated the law.

2. Equally important is that portion of the prospectus entitled "Risk Factors" or "Special Considerations," or something similar. All of the risks associated with the investment are itemized here. For example, you will find out in this section how far along a company's product development might be, or the fact that management has borrowed a good deal of money from other sources.

Other important items you'll want to look for here include:

• Whether or not the partnership is dealing in properties that are already identified. Sometimes, partnerships will collect money first and then find properties in which to invest. As an investor, you should steer clear of these kinds of partnerships.

• It is also important that you ascertain whether or not "leverage," or borrowed money, is to be used to purchase the properties. The use of leverage can cut down on your overall return.

• Are any guarantees being made as far as returns are concerned? If so, what kinds of guarantees are there?

It is vital that you read and understand every word in the risk section, which is the area that the registered rep or salesperson may have avoided when discussing this opportunity with you.

3. There is always a section describing the management of the business. Here, track record and credibility in the field are the most important factors. If any of the executives have had lawsuits filed against them or have experienced difficulties with other deals, that will be revealed in this section.

4. Conflicts of interest. If the managers have any conflicts of interest, they must be detailed in this section. An example of a conflict of interest is buying properties from other entities owned or controlled by the general partners, or other financial dealings that would directly affect the operation of the partnership.

5. Expert opinions. Every prospectus has to contain a legal and accounting opinion. Do your best to understand these opinions. Do not be unduly impressed if the opinion is rendered by a well-known accounting or legal firm. Some of them have been sued successfully for rendering sloppy opinions. The firms are retained and paid by the company issuing the security. They are interested mainly in whether the prospectus conforms to certain guidelines. For example, the accountant's job is to ascertain whether all financial statements and projections are in accord with "generally accepted accounting principles." They are therefore guaranteeing not that the information provided is correct but rather that the auditor has found nothing to show that the information is *not* correct.

These firms, however, can only work with the information supplied to them by the security issuer. Facts and data that can be relevant to the offering might be withheld. All relevant information should be uncovered by the legal and accounting firms, but the reality is that they often are working under time constraints and with the data they are given. It may be extremely difficult, therefore, for the lawyers and accountants to uncover cleverly disguised fraudulent acts.

Prospectuses, then, should not be looked upon as flawless documents, although they normally do an excellent job of pointing out the risks and advantages. Information can be and sometimes is skewed toward marketing the security. Although prospectuses are essentially disclosure documents, it is very possible that some aspects of the investment have not been disclosed or are disclosed in a way that makes them appear harmless.

Wise investors use prospectuses as sources of information about an investment, but they don't use them as measures of the worth of the investment.

When considering a partnership, the investor should be particularly wary. The Investment Partnership Association, the advocate for the partnership industry, has prepared a checklist to help investors evaluate and choose a partnership investment. The checklist follows:

• What is the general economic outlook in the industry in which the partnership will be operating?

• Does the partnership plan for downturns in its industry or in the economy in general?

• Does the sponsor (general partner) have a management track record and experience in the industry in which the limited partnership is being developed?

• What is the potential for total capital appreciation of the limited partnership?

• Are there additional benefits, such as tax deductions or sheltering of income during the life of the partnership?

• Does the partnership guarantee a minimum amount of cash distribution or capital gains of the underlying businesses?

• Will regular reports on the program's performance be provided to the investors?

• Is the investor able to sell his or her interest back to the partnership during the life of the program, and if so, how will the price be determined?

• How much leverage will be used in the partnership? If so, are the loans non-recourse to investors, and how accurate are financial forecasts for repayment of the debt?

• How are the income and capital gains to be distributed among the partners, and how much of the investor's money is going into the acquisition and management of the assets?

Working with Your Broker

Investing is difficult and risky. You need all the help you can get. You should look at your broker as your partner in the investment process. No matter how confident or sophisticated you are, two heads are always better than one. Even investors who do their own research find that a highly skilled and experienced broker who can challenge assumptions or with whom they can exchange ideas is a valuable resource.

You should take some responsibility for your own decision-making, even while you receive input from your investment professional. A topflight broker should be able to sift through the mounds of information available and point you in the right direction. But a broker may have hundreds of clients, and it is a tough chore keeping up with the needs and desires of all of them. You have to expect, therefore, to do some things on your own.

What constitutes a good working relationship with a broker? Communication is the most important factor. You should be in contact whenever there is a problem.

If you have a great deal of faith in your broker's financial acumen, consult him or her regularly. But don't take things for granted; check on the results of your broker's decisions as quickly and as often as possible.

Some experienced and savvy investors feel that all they need is a discount broker to execute trades for them. But they probably spend much of their free time studying the markets from all angles, and they subscribe to every investment newsletter and read every newspaper they can get their hands on. If you are not this type of person, you may well prefer a broker who works for a full-service firm that can provide you with ideas that you don't have the time to research yourself.

Evaluating Your Broker

Once you have selected a competent, honest broker, how do you know whether he or she is doing a good job for you? Here are some guidelines:

• The only reason to take on the risks of investing is to earn a better return than you can get at a bank. If the economy and the investment climate have been healthy, there's no reason why your broker can't help you obtain a higher rate of return. If your broker hasn't been able to do that within a year's time, you should find out why.

• Have you kept pace with market averages? For example, if the Standard & Poor's 500 stock average has advanced 15 percent over the past six months, have you done approximately that well? If not, investigate the situation.

• Are you paying too much in commissions for what you are earning? If you would have had an 18 percent return but your commission costs were 15 percent, you actually earned only 3 percent. If that's the case, your broker may be recommending too many short-term trades.

• Does the broker recommend only proprietary products? If so, find out why and ask if there are other products that are just as suitable. Undue dependence on in-house products could indicate that the broker is more interested in winning contests than in earning money for you and protecting your interests.

• Does your broker advise you only to buy and never to sell? That may be fine if you own nothing but blue-chip securities or you are a very long-term investor, but in any case, the matter is a good one to discuss with your broker.

• How do your investments rate with Standard & Poor's or Moody's? Ask your broker for a written report on the Standard & Poor's or Moody's ratings on your securities, or go to your local library and check the ratings yourself. If you see that you have a lot of substandard investments, the broker may be taking more chances with your money than you want.

• Has the broker tried to assume full control of all investment decisions without your permission? If so, complain immediately. Even if you have made money, the broker is acting dishonestly.

• Is the broker keeping you properly apprised of significant developments, both positive and negative, concerning your portfolio? You shouldn't have to find out something about one of your investments two or three weeks after it has taken place. A good broker will be on top of what's happening to your securities.

• Are you meeting all your financial goals in a manner that is consistent with your risk profile?

• Is the broker difficult or impossible to reach when things are going badly? A broker should be in touch with you in good times and bad. This doesn't mean that your broker should hold your hand, but he or she should be available when you have to make tough decisions.

9 · INVESTOR PROTECTION

At every step along the investment road, rules and regulations have been put in place to protect the individual small investor from being duped.

Many years ago, our lawmakers recognized that since investors provide the seed money for most corporate and governmental initiatives, it is vital that these investors have confidence in the money-raising system. If that system is seen as fundamentally flawed, investors will lose confidence, and little if any money will be raised to keep the economy going.

To ensure confidence, then, the federal and state governments, through various regulatory bodies, have set up an elaborate network of investor protection that normally works quite well. However, the network does fail from time to time.

Individuals who invest in publicly traded securities are protected by five layers of laws, rules, and regulations that complement one another:

1. Federal laws, specifically the Securities Act of 1933 and the Securities Exchange Act of 1934
2. Rules and regulations of the Securities and Exchange Commission (SEC)

3. State blue-sky laws, which protect state residents against certain unethical and illegal practices
4. Rules and regulations of the various stock exchanges and the National Association of Securities Dealers (NASD)
5. In addition, internal broker-dealer compliance rules must be followed.

Several of these entities have the power to fine offending companies and to enforce other sanctions. It must be emphasized that the SEC does not approve or disapprove of securities, nor does it make any representation as to a security's value or risk. Its only job is to make sure that you have all the information you need to make a sound investment decision.

Some security offerings do not have to be registered. For example, private placement offerings, which are sold only to a limited number of sophisticated investors, are exempt from registration, as are municipal, state, and federal bonds and offerings of small business investment companies (SBICs). Commodities are not classified as securities, and the SEC has no jurisdiction over commodity markets or brokers who buy and sell commodities and nothing else. The commodities markets are regulated by the Commodities Futures Trading Commission (CFTC).

The Securities Act of 1933 was a historic and important piece of consumer protection legislation. However, it addresses mainly problems that might arise between investors and public companies that issue securities. The Securities Exchange Act of 1934 mainly addresses broker–client relations.

The Securities Exchange Act of 1934

The Securities Exchange Act of 1934 regulates the behavior of registered representatives vis-à-vis their clients, so it is of great concern to individual investors. This law also makes full disclosure a requirement of securities listed and registered for public trading on securities exchanges. In 1964, these requirements were extended to over-the-counter securities.

The 1934 law also:

• Enumerates specific prohibited trading and sales practices of registered representatives and broker-dealers
• Requires registration of broker-dealers
• Details margin trading rules and restrictions
• Prohibits insider trading
• Regulates the solicitation of proxies
• Requires that broker-dealers file management and financial information with the SEC and provide annual updates

The Securities and Exchange Commission (SEC)

The **Securities and Exchange Commission** is the federal government's ultimate investor watchdog. Although the members of the SEC are appointed by the president, the agency's mission is a nonpolitical one—investor protection. The SEC's purpose is to ensure that all investors get a fair shake from the securities markets themselves and from the firms and their brokers who sell securities. Not only do public companies that issue securities have to register them with the SEC, but broker-dealers who buy and sell them on behalf of investors have to register as well. This means that *all* broker-dealers must comply with *all* SEC regulations.

The SEC is vested with enforcement powers that it exercises frequently. For example, when a number of Wall Street bigwigs were prosecuted in the late 1980s for insider trading, the SEC played an important role in bringing them to justice. The SEC prosecutes high-profile cases in order to assure the public that the investment process will be as fair as possible. The SEC does not, however, collect money for or award damages to individual investors who have been defrauded by a broker. Such investors can recover only by suing in a court of law or by bringing an arbitration proceeding. Rather than getting involved in the nitty-gritty of investor protection, the SEC views itself as responsible for the big picture. It defines its role this way:

> The SEC's principal objectives are to make sure the securities markets operate in a fair and orderly manner, that securities industry professionals deal justly with their customers, and that corporations make public all information about themselves that investors need to make intelligent investment decisions. The SEC pursues these objectives by overseeing the operation of the SROs [self-regulatory organizations, such as the New York Stock Exchange and the National Association of Securities Dealers], adopting rules with which those involved in the purchase and sale of securities must comply, and filing lawsuits or taking other enforcement action in cases where the law has been violated.

Blue-Sky Laws

Even though the SEC has national jurisdiction with regard to securities-law violations, each state has its own securities department that is responsible for protecting state residents from securities fraud. State securities departments can and often do prohibit some securities from being sold in their particular state. State laws regulating securities sales are referred to collectively as **blue-sky laws**.

The state securities regulators are all members of the North American Securities Administrators Association (NASAA), which provides a reliable source of information for the nation's top state securities regulators. These state regulators may take on the smaller cases that the SEC will not or cannot handle. For example, if you are defrauded of $10,000 by a broker, state regulators might investigate, rather than the SEC. Nevertheless, federal and state securities laws often overlap, and it is not unusual for a firm or a registered representative to be subject to penalties in both federal and state courts.

The National Association of Securities Dealers

Congress decided that the SEC's role was primarily that of an overseer, and the securities industry should, to the best of its ability, regulate itself. The industry responded to the challenge by establishing the **National Association of Securities Dealers** (NASD). Besides being the main regulatory body for the industry, it is also the chief licensing group. Any broker-dealer, broker, or registered representative who sells publicly traded securities must be licensed by the NASD. *If a registered rep or a broker-dealer cannot present you with proof of registration with the NASD, do not do business with him or her.*

The NASD has the power to fine, censure, suspend licenses, and ultimately bar from the business registered representatives and broker-dealers who commit violations. Essentially, Congress and the SEC make the rules and regulations and, except for extreme cases, the NASD enforces them. The NASD also makes its own rules, which must be approved by the SEC.

Broker-Dealer Enforcement

The weakest link in the customer-protection chain is the broker-dealer. These firms are supposed to be the first line of defense against broker wrongdoing, since they must enforce all NASD and SEC rules, but they have an inherent conflict of interest. These firms employ the brokers and they make money from their efforts, so enforcement at the broker-dealer level tends to be spotty at best.

Most broker-dealers have a compliance officer assigned to monitor customer accounts and to work with any brokers who are having problems in the area of investor protection. These officers—often attorneys experienced in negotiating settlements—try to resolve problems before they become court cases.

It is the firm's branch manager, however, who is initially responsible for all broker conduct, supervision, and investment protection. Branch managers may be reluctant to discipline a broker, especially one who is a big producer, and this problem can be exacerbated when the branch manager is compensated with an override (or extra pay) based on the production of each broker in the branch.

Some broker-dealers engage in conduct that, although not illegal, is unfair. For example, one large brokerage firm made some unprofitable investments for its own account in the cellular phone industry. The firm's management decided to try to recoup those losses by packaging all of these bad investments into a limited partnership that it would sell to unwitting clients. In other words, clients were being offered investments that already had failed.

Some critics have characterized broker-dealer enforcement as equivalent to leaving the fox in charge of the henhouse.

Negative-Consent Letters

The letter shown on page 82 appears innocuous. But **negative-consent** or activity letters are far from harmless. If you sign and return such a letter, *you could lose your right to get your money back in case of a violation of one of your investor's rights.*

This letter probably came from the surveillance unit of the broker-dealer, although it is signed by the branch manager. Why the surveillance unit? It could be that in looking over trading activity for the day, that unit detected what it thought could be a violation in your account, such as an unsuitable trade or a high-risk trading strategy.

Although the letter obfuscates its actual purpose, the firm wants to confirm that you, as a customer, have in fact agreed to broker conduct that appears problematical. By signing, you are consenting to the action, and if you should later sue or go to arbitration on this transaction, the firm can produce the signed letter to show that you agreed to it.

Don't sign such a letter and don't call your broker to ask about it. Instead, immediately call the person who wrote the letter and ask for details about why it was sent. It could be routine, but be wary.

SIPC Protection

Most broker-dealers in the United States are members of the **Securities Investor Protection Corporation** (SIPC). Similar to the FDIC for banks and savings and loans, it provides some insurance if your broker-dealer fails financially and is unable to meet its obligation to you.

If your broker-dealer should become bankrupt and it has SIPC protection, you get back all securities held by the firm in your name or in the process of being registered. Your account is insured up to $500,000, including up to $100,000 of cash held in a brokerage account.

The SIPC defines securities as stocks, bonds, notes, and certificates of deposit that are held by customers. It omits, however, commodity interests, contracts, or options.

The SIPC offers some protection for the value of your investments, but only if a securities firm should go bankrupt. It does not cover a decline in the market value of securities in your portfolio. It does not cover losses caused by a broker's fraud or negligence.

Caveat Emptor

Despite all of the investor protection described above, investors continue to be defrauded by unscrupulous financial professionals who slip through the cracks of the regulatory processes. That means that the burden of protecting your investments ultimately

October 15, 1990

Dear Client:

As part of my regular duties, I routinely review many accounts in the office. In conducting this review, I have found that your account is one of our most valuable ones. I would like to take this opportunity to thank you for favoring us with your patronage. It is our hope that we can always please you.

In the current investment climate, I feel that it is prudent for all investors to periodically review their investment goals and the financial resources available to attain those goals. This review might consider factors such as degree of trading risk assumed, commission costs associated with active accounts, and resulting tax consequences.

Please take this as an opportunity to review your investment objectives and all of the factors that may influence them. I would appreciate your signing and returning the lower portion of this letter as an indication that you have reviewed your investment program.

We appreciate this opportunity to be of service to you.

Sincerely,

Hugo Bidemeyer, Manager

- -

This will confirm that the activity in my account is in full accordance with my investment objectives and authorization in full consideration of the risks and costs associated with such activity.

_____   _____

Signature   Signature

falls on you. Approach every transaction with the attitude of "buyer beware."

There are a number of steps you can take to protect yourself:

• Always think of an investment as a business transaction and treat it as such. That means using caution and common sense.

• Diversify your investments; don't put all your eggs in one basket. Use the financial pyramid as your example.

• Maintain full control over your own financial affairs. Don't cede that control to anyone, no matter how expert he or she appears to be.

• Don't rush. There is no investment opportunity that can't wait until tomorrow.

• A hot tip is exactly that. You probably will end up being burned.

• Registered representatives, brokers, or whatever they call themselves are salespeople who make money by trading securities.

• There are no guarantees.

The two most important watchwords for every investor are *awareness* and *prudence*. Be aware of what's going on at all times in your account and exercise prudence in managing your account.

Before you invest:

• If you are in doubt about a recommendation from your broker, *ask the broker to put in writing his or her statement that a particular investment is suitable for you.* And seek further information—from your broker or other sources. Never invest in something you don't understand.

• Ask for the firm's research report on that security.

• Ask for the Standard & Poor's and Moody's ratings for the security.

• Ask for articles from *The Wall Street Journal, Barron's, Forbes, Fortune, Business Week,* or other recognized newspapers or magazines concerning the investment and the company that is issuing it. Do the articles confirm your broker's advice? If this is a new issue, carefully read the risk portion of the prospectus that must be given to you.

• Finally, IF YOU DON'T UNDERSTAND, DON'T BUY.

10 · COMMON ABUSES

There are many ways in which a broker can violate his or her fiduciary responsibility. Some of the most common ones are explained in this chapter. Options for handling complaints are detailed in chapter 11.

Churning

Churning, a very common practice, means overtrading an account for the purpose of generating more commissions. In other words, a broker will, without justification and sometimes without your permission, make a multitude of trades that bear little or no relation to your goals.

Full-service broker-dealers are most vulnerable to the temptation to churn your account. Discount brokers, who make no recommendations and take directions only from you, do not have such temptations. However, it is unwise for a novice investor to deal with a discount broker. An honest, full-service registered representative knows a lot more about investing than you do and should know what investments are suitable. At a discount brokerage, no one is there to advise you.

It's possible that even if your account has been churned, you can turn a profit. But if your account hadn't been churned, your profit might have been higher. It is easier for a broker to churn an account when the stock market is rising because you probably are focusing on the bottom line, not on how much is going out in commissions. Any registered rep who engages in churning, no matter what the ultimate effect on your account, has committed a violation of the securities laws.

Check your monthly brokerage statements carefully and look for unauthorized trades or unaccustomed activity in your account. That is the quickest way to spot churning.

Mutual-Fund Trading

Mutual funds—especially those with loads (sales charges)—are not meant to be traded regularly. If you purchase a mutual fund with a load from your broker, and a short time later he or she tries to convince you to sell that fund and replace it with another load fund, this is similar to churning, and it, too, is a violation. A convincing argument could be made that the only reason the broker switched you from one load fund to another was to earn the commission on the second fund. Mutual funds generally are supposed to be long-term holds.

There is no rule of thumb for how long you should keep a mutual fund, but if you want to make a change, it should be your decision, not your registered rep's—after a full investigation of the costs of and reasons for the change.

Unauthorized Trading

Unauthorized trading involves a broker making trades without permission. Sometimes this occurs when the investor is out of touch with the broker and the broker assumes that the trade would have been authorized if the investor were available to give permission. Nevertheless, the broker has violated his or her fiduciary duty.

Scrutinize every trade that appears on your confirmations and monthly statements. Complain immediately if there is an unauthorized transaction. The temptation to churn the account or to make unauthorized trades is great.

Unauthorized Accounts

The establishment of any account by the registered representative without your authorization constitutes another violation of the securities laws. Managed accounts, discretionary accounts, options accounts, commodity accounts, and margin accounts require your *written* authorization. If you must give discretionary powers to a registered rep, notify the branch manager at the same time.

Disobeying Instructions

If a registered representative fails to follow your legitimate instructions, a violation of the securities laws has occurred. For example, if you asked your broker to put a stop loss order on a stock and it was not done, whether or not it was the registered rep's fault (it might have been a back-office foul-up), you have the right to seek redress.

Here again, your best proof is a copy of your written instructions specifying in detail exactly what you wanted done. Don't depend on telephone or oral instructions alone.

Commissions

This generally works out in the range of 1 to 3 percent, although there are exceptions. Stock commission rates are based on round-lot trades—that is, on multiples of 100 shares. Broker-dealers may have varying commission rates for bonds or odd lots (under-100-share groups). When you check your statements and confirmations for commission charges, any commission that you are charged above the agreed rate should be brought to the immediate attention of your broker.

Markups

When a security is listed on an exchange, its price is determined by the auction process described in chapter 6. However, the prices of unlisted securities—those traded on the over-the-counter market—are determined in a different way. If, for example, you want to buy an over-the-counter security, the broker-dealer is legally bound to go out and find the security at the best price available from another dealer.

Certain brokers "make a market" in specified OTC products. This means that the broker-dealer keeps shares of the security on hand and can sell them at a price it deems fair at a given point in time.

Market makers obtain their securities from sellers and then may hold on to them for some period of time until they can make a profit by selling. For instance, assume that XYZ brokerage firm buys 1,000 shares of ABC stock at $1 a share on July 1. XYZ is a market maker in ABC. XYZ might have an immediate buyer for the stock who is willing to pay $1.03 per share. XYZ probably will sell the stock for that price and make 3 cents a share on the sale. The 3 cents is the **markup.**

If, however, there is no immediate buyer, XYZ can put the stock "on the shelf" and wait until a buyer comes along who is willing to purchase the stock for more than XYZ paid for it.

It is possible that one of XYZ's regular customers may want to buy ABC at some point, especially if XYZ's registered reps are pushing it. When that happens, XYZ quotes a price, and, if it is acceptable to the customer, a deal is struck. According to the securities laws, markups must be fair. What is fair? NASD rules state that generally a markup may be no more than 5 percent over the price XYZ paid for the stock.

If you buy an over-the-counter security, you have the right to know whether your broker-dealer is a market maker in the security, and, if so, what the markup is. You may be given an evasive or wrong answer; you can't know for sure. What you can do, though, is to ask the registered rep to include the amount of the markup in your written confirmation. An honest confirmation will state clearly that the broker-dealer was either a "principal" or a "market maker" in this transaction, and it will include the amount of the markup. If the rep refuses or the information you requested does not appear on the confirmation, it's possible that the rep and the broker-dealer are hiding something.

Many of the problems associated with penny-stock scam artists in recent years have been related to excessive markups. These dishonest firms manipulated the markups by buying from and selling to their own customers, inflating the markup with each sale.

Misrepresentation

Harry was an avid golfer who played golf every day after he retired. One of his golfing buddies told him about a "hotshot" broker who seemed to know everything there was to know about stocks in the retailing sector of the economy. Harry had never been an investor, but his career had been in the retail business, and he still had a "love affair with retailing." However, since he had retired, he had lost touch with the business, and many of his former colleagues also had retired. Harry went to talk to the broker, whose name was Stan. Stan told Harry, "I am a specialist in retailing stocks. I have been following the industry for ten years and I know everybody in the business." When he mentioned a number of prominent names, Harry was impressed, and he invested $50,000 with Stan almost immediately.

Stan, however, turned out to be a con artist. He knew very little about the retailing business and had picked up the names he used from articles he had read in retail trade journals and other financial papers. Needless to say, Harry lost most of his $50,000.

If a registered representative claims to have special knowledge of a type of security or a group of companies when in fact he or she does not, that is a violation of the securities laws. Ask for proof of any alleged expertise. Being quoted in a magazine or newspaper article is a start, but don't settle for that. Ask for references of other investors who have had success trading in the broker's specialty.

Misrepresentation can also involve the omission of a salient fact about a security or a strategy. For example, if you are not told that a company whose stock you are buying recently underwent reorganization under the bankruptcy laws—which of course increases the risks of the stock—that also constitutes a securities violation. As an aggrieved investor, you have the right to seek redress against the broker and the broker-dealer.

Guarantees Against Loss

All investments carry some risk, and any broker who assures you that you can't lose on a particular investment has violated his or her fiduciary duty of truthfulness. Similarly, neither can the registered representative's employer, the broker-dealer, make a loss guarantee. If, for example, a brokerage firm advertises that a fund investing in GNMA (Government National Mortgage Association, or Ginnie Mae) bonds provides investors with 100 percent safety of principal and a guaranteed rate of return "because of a federal government guarantee"—which it does not have—it has broken the law.

Failure to Inform of All Risks

One of a broker's major duties is to let you know all the risks associated with a recommended investment. To sell a product, a registered rep may be tempted not to mention all its risks. Junk bonds—high-risk corporate bonds that have been used in leveraged buyouts—are an example. In recent years, many investors have lost a great deal of money on them.

Sales Puffing

A common sales technique is to puff up or make something appear to be more valuable than it is. The broker might say, "This stock will undoubtedly double in a month" or "I can assure you that this will reach $25." There is no way that these statements can be proved, yet many investors will take them at face value.

The most famous line has got to be, "I have put my own money into this investment." That may indeed be true, but how can you prove it? And even if it is so, there is still no guarantee that you will make a profit.

Violations of Trust

Registered reps are fiduciaries, and they are supposed to do what is best for you. From time to time, a broker may do something or neglect to do something that is a violation of the fiduciary duty of trust, even though it is not a violation of any law or regulation. For example, there is nothing wrong with a broker recommending a stock, but if a high-grade bond, which probably is a safer investment, would achieve the same ends and goals, the bond should be recommended. However, because the commission may be smaller on a bond than on a stock, the broker may not even mention the bond. In this case, the broker did not violate any regulation, but he or she has not done his or her fiduciary duty, and you have the right to have that wrong redressed.

Refusing Orders

There are times when your broker should refuse your order. If you request a transaction that is unsuitable and highly risky—

penny stocks, certain high-risk options, or some commodity transactions, for example, when you have stated that your investment goal is steady income—it is the duty of your registered rep to turn down that request.

It is the duty of the broker, again acting as a fiduciary, to recommend more suitable alternative investments. Even if you balk and threaten to take your business elsewhere, the registered rep should act properly by refusing the business.

Other Prohibited Practices

A registered rep may not buy or sell one product dependent on the purchase or sale of another. Some reps may try to sell you something at a discount but insist that you buy some other product at full price as part of the deal.

Also, the broker is prohibited from misrepresenting the nature of the tax benefits of a particular investment. Similarly, your broker as an individual is banned from lending money (for a margin transaction) or securities (for a short-sale transaction) to you or borrowing money or securities from you.

The Options Temptation

A stock option is defined as a right that takes the form of a contract to buy or sell a given number of shares of a specified stock at a fixed price within a predetermined time period.

"Options fever" is a disease that afflicts those brokers who let greed get the best of them. Because most options strategies require many trades, a broker can make some nice commissions by convincing you to buy and sell options. The dishonest broker usually doesn't mention all the risks involved in stock options.

What makes options so risky is that by utilizing certain option strategies (and there are many), you can actually lose *more* than your investment in the option. Furthermore, certain kinds of options necessitate your having a margin account, and you might well be subject to a margin call.

Registered reps are not naïve about the risks of options. Even some of the industry terminology reflects a certain cynicism. For instance, one term used universally is *alligator spread*. This is not a real options strategy but a series of transactions in the options market that "eats the investor alive" with commissions. According to *Barron's Dictionary of Finance and Investment Terms*, the term *alligator spread* is used "when a broker arranges a combination of puts and calls that generates so much commission the client is unlikely to turn a profit even if the markets move as anticipated." Real options strategies include the "butterfly spread" and the "diagonal spread." These are very complex techniques used by only the most savvy of options traders.

Insider Trading

Although the average individual investor will rarely come in contact with insider trading, it has become such a well-publicized phenomenon that it should be discussed here.

Insider trading usually involves an executive, director, or major shareholder of a company, or a person who owes a fiduciary duty to a company and is privy to its confidential plans. Such a person may know in advance about a development that will cause the company's stock either to rise or to fall, and he or she uses this information to make a profit on the purchase or sale of the stock. Other people far removed from a company may also be guilty of insider trading if they knowingly accept and act upon nonpublic information received from insiders.

The securities laws prohibit company insiders from profiting from information about which the general public is unaware. For example, if an executive of XYZ company knows that XYZ soon will be merging with ABC company, but nobody outside the company knows it, that executive cannot buy shares of XYZ or ABC stock prior to the public announcement of the merger. Or if that same executive knows that XYZ will be reporting a loss for the quarter, he or she is barred from selling shares of

XYZ before the loss is made public. Nor can the executive pass on the inside information to a relative or even a friend.

The reasoning behind this rule, as with many securities rules and laws, is that such an action gives the insider an unfair advantage over the ordinary investor.

Every once in a while, a broker will try to convince you to buy stock on the basis of information obtained from somebody "close to the company" or "inside the company." Such claims, of course, should be dismissed out of hand. He or she probably is lying. If the broker truly had inside information, why would he or she tell you, a complete stranger? And even if his or her information were accurate, you would be violating the law by acting on it.

Broker-Dealer Violations

Ultimately, it is the broker-dealer who is responsible if a violation occurs. A firm hires the registered representatives who work for it, and the company therefore is responsible for its employees' actions. But these firms also have a direct duty to investors. Branch managers, for example, must periodically review the trading in all accounts to see that the trades fit the customers' suitability guidelines. If the manager fails to spot a problem that is a violation of the securities laws, that failure constitutes a lack of proper supervision, for which the firm can be held liable.

Record of Complaints

All broker-dealers must maintain a file of customer complaints. This file is audited periodically by the stock exchanges and the NASD to be sure that the broker-dealer is following up on them. If a number of complaints have been lodged against one registered representative, the broker-dealer must investigate thoroughly. If during the audit, the stock exchange or the NASD notices a pattern of complaints against a particular rep, it can initiate an investigation on its own, even though no customer has filed a complaint to the regulatory body. This is designed to weed out the bad apples in the industry. However, if a registered representative is a big producer for a broker-dealer, the firm is likely to be reluctant to act swiftly on complaints. You can't assume, therefore, that the broker-dealers are always doing their compliance job well. If you feel that a wrong has been committed against you, you must act aggressively to right it.

Central Records Depository

The SEC, SROs, state regulatory authorities, and the **North American Securities Administrators Association** (NASAA) maintain the **Central Records Depository**, a computerized data base of disciplinary records on individual brokers. The information stored there is obtained from the broker-dealers and registered reps themselves, without the use of any consistent reporting standard. It is possible, therefore, that some disciplinary actions taken against a particular broker might not be included. However, it is better than no data base at all.

The Penny-Stock Problem

There are a small group of broker-dealers who specialize in the sale of **penny stocks**—risky, low-priced stocks that generally cost less than $1 per share. Many are start-up companies. Some are mining outfits operating on a wing and a prayer; some are companies based on an unproven invention; and some are merely corporate shells, with no operating business whatever. All are highly speculative investments. For the most part, the companies that issue these stocks have little or no track record, and, as a result, they are difficult to analyze. Unfortunately, some broker-dealers have perpetrated various scams on potential buyers by selling stocks in these companies. The SEC, the NASD, and state regulatory authorities have recently been cracking down on these swindlers.

For the most part, companies that issue penny stocks (strictly speaking, stocks that sell for $5 or less, although many sell for literally pennies a share) do so because they have no other source of financing. Since they are newly established companies, banks and venture capitalists may not want to lend them money, so they turn to the general public. Their products or services are often in the developmental stages, and they probably have not yet earned a profit.

Investors often are attracted to these stocks because they are affordable, and if a company does well, the investment can triple or quadruple quite quickly. Thus, investors dream of big profits—even though those profits don't often materialize. Some broker-dealers take advantage of such greedy fantasies to bilk investors.

For instance, in a recent case, investors were talked into buying shares in a company based in Australia that bred cattle. The brokers worked in a new firm that formerly had operated under a different name and had been prosecuted for defrauding investors. As was typical in these situations, the broker-dealer "made a market" in the shares of the Australian company: The broker-dealer took almost all of the stock issue for itself and charged the customers whatever price it could get. When the customers realized they were losing money and wanted to sell, they found that there were no buyers. Since the stock was traded only by this one company, there was no other market for the shares.

It must be understood clearly that in the great majority of these situations, it is not the company issuing the stock that is at fault—it is the broker-dealer that defrauds the unwary investor. An honest broker-dealer maintains a market by ensuring that enough buyers and sellers are involved in the transaction so that the stock can be fairly traded.

The SEC has issued the following statement about penny-stock fraud:

> While there are risks with any investment, the following risks are particularly great with penny stocks:

• Risk of market domination and price manipulation. Many penny stocks are traded by a single brokerage firm, or just a few firms. When a stock is traded by a single broker, or a single broker controls most of the market, that broker has a monopoly and could take unfair advantage of you by manipulating market prices. While many broker-dealers handling penny stocks are honest, these stocks still represent a considerable risk to the investor.

• Risk of being overcharged. Brokerage firms that sell penny stocks generally earn their profits on these sales by overcharging you a markup above the price the firm is paying for the stock. The NASD generally sets limits on markups. Undisclosed, excessive markups are illegal. Some firms sell penny stocks with undisclosed markups of 100 percent or more. Because of the limited number of firms trading any one penny stock and the limited availability of current price information, the opportunity for unscrupulous brokerage firms to overcharge you is a particular problem.

• Lack of stock price information. Frequently, it will be difficult or impossible for you to use sources other than your broker to monitor your broker's recommendations or changes in the value of your investment.

• Lack of information about your investment. Companies with stock traded on an exchange or quoted on NASDAQ are required to make quarterly and annual reports publicly available. Some penny stock companies distribute quarterly and annual reports, but many do not.

A particularly pernicious practice is the **"boiler-room operation"** promoting penny stocks. Thousands of people have been bilked out of millions of dollars in these schemes, which occur in a similar pattern time and time again.

The scenario is familiar. You are just sitting down to dinner and the phone rings. A friendly voice greets you warmly and identifies himself or herself as Mr. or Ms. So-and-So from such-and-such brokerage firm.

The caller (nowadays known as a telemarketer) will ask you if you know anything about the exciting world of new emerging growth companies, then the caller will go on to tell you that his or her firm is in the forefront of taking quality companies public. The caller claims that he or she personally meets with the management of these companies, and that the firm allegedly has done excellent research on them. The caller then will ask if you are interested in hearing more about such opportunities. Even if you say no, you probably will receive another call a few days or a few weeks later.

The next time, the caller mentions that he or she is "working on a deal" and asks whether you would mind another call. Even if you say no, they will call again. Such salespeople are nothing if not persistent.

The third call usually is the sales pitch. The caller sounds very enthusiastic about some unique product or service sold by whatever company he or she is touting. The story sounds plausible and the stock is dirt cheap—say, $3 a share—but "you must act immediately" or "you can't wait" or "you must send in your check today," because other clients will want this stock, and only so much of it is available. You are then asked to buy a large amount, such as 5,000 shares, for "only $15,000."

If you don't bite at this point, the caller will become more aggressive and tell you that this is a "can't-miss" situation and "it's deals like this that make the rich richer." He or she may even "personally guarantee" that the stock will double in a short time and that you will realize a hefty profit.

If you don't buy after all the hard sell, he or she will call you again in a few weeks with another "can't-miss opportunity" and add, "By the way, that stock I told you about a few weeks ago has now tripled in value." But the caller will assure you that this new one will do just as well—and the cycle begins all over again.

Many people have received these calls, and unfortunately many have fallen for the scam. The spiel may not always be just for penny stocks—it may be for strategic metals, commodities, high-priced stocks, mutual funds, and/or limited partnerships. These boiler-room operators may lead you to believe that they are legitimate broker-dealers, but in fact they are not.

Surprisingly, intelligent people fall for such scams. But you never will, as long as you remember two basic rules of investing: (1) Never be rushed into making a decision; and (2) always insist on studying written material (including a prospectus or an annual report) before you invest. Never buy any investment based only on a telephone pitch.

In addition, as discussed earlier in this book, you should always check out the seller as well as the security being offered. The last thing you want is a boiler-room broker.

Futures and Metals Scams

Penny stockbrokers are not the only ones working the phones these days. People from licensed commodities futures firms are calling naïve investors and talking them into buying Eurodollars, gold and other metals, and pork bellies.

Like their penny-stock counterparts, these brokers are promising high returns and not mentioning the extremely high risks associated with futures trading or the enormous commissions they are charging—which have been as high as 40 percent of the transaction price. To make matters worse, these brokers sometimes induce customers to finance their purchases with bank loans arranged by the broker-dealers. Not only are you hit with large interest charges of approximately 12 percent on the loans, but you also are charged commissions of 3 to 4 percent for the buying or selling. This means that the investment must earn 18 to 20 percent before you see any profit. And because funds are leveraged to pay for the investment, any losses incurred will be greater than if it had been an all-cash transaction. It is almost impossible to make money under these circumstances.

Protecting Yourself

There are legitimate brokers of stocks, commodities, and strategic metals, and many of them use the telephone to solicit customers. You shouldn't assume that because you are called on the phone, it is a scam—just don't ever buy as a result of that phone call alone.

Protect yourself by following some simple rules—ones that have universal application and should be applied to all dealings with brokers:

• Ask to see specific research information about the investment. The dishonest broker will send a slick brochure that talks in generalities about an investment; a legitimate operator will be more than happy to send you detailed information.

• Check out the broker and his or her firm with the NASD, your local SEC office, or your state securities bureau.

• Don't be stampeded into buying an investment. Before you send any money, consult with an adviser or a financially savvy friend or acquaintance. There is nothing that can't wait until tomorrow.

• Have the broker send you information about the investment from a source outside of his firm, such as a recent newspaper or magazine article from a widely recognized publication. This is especially important if the broker is claiming that some "miracle breakthrough" has occurred.

• Never purchase an investment from somebody until you have met him or her face-to-face.

• Be skeptical of anyone who promises you quick profits. Investments rarely work that way.

• Never buy from a broker who doesn't try to "qualify you" by asking about your experience as an investor and your investment goals.

• Remember that no investments come with a guarantee.

• Don't assume that a registered rep is an expert on life insurance or some other product that is not a security, even if he or she is licensed to sell it.

• Remember that no matter what the name—account executive, registered representative, financial consultant, investment counselor, or broker—all such financial professionals are primarily salespeople.

• Never give up control over your account to your broker, no matter how competent or trustworthy he or she may appear to be.

Investors' Legal Rights

Once you open an account with a broker-dealer, you are entitled to the following:

• The right to expect that each and every trade will be executed promptly and that the broker will use all reasonable means to secure the best price

• The right to a written confirmation of all executed trades, including information about the date of the transaction, the identity of the security bought or sold, and the number of shares, units, or principal amount of the security

• The right to receive from the broker-dealer disclosure as to the cost of the actual transaction, including commissions charged

• The right not to be misled

If a broker-dealer violates any of these rights, even in a minor way, you are entitled to compensation for any losses that resulted from the violation.

The right to honest and trustworthy recommendations and advice. Your broker should be a truly professional financial adviser who considers your financial goals and financial capabilities above all else. When Christine O'Reilly asked her broker for a recommendation, he advised her to invest in his firm's "stock of the week," a speculative offering that was not at all suitable for this young widow who had children to educate. By not considering Christine's conservative goals in making the recommendation, the broker was violating her rights.

The right to have your interests as a customer come first. This should be true even when your interests and those of the broker or broker-dealer are in conflict. For example, if you and the broker-dealer have invested in a security that is falling, you should be given the opportunity to get out of the investment before the firm does so. You have the right to the higher price. Steve Mapes was very surprised when the stock he had purchased on the advice of his broker took a sudden tumble. He later found out that the broker-dealer with whom he was doing business "made a market" in the stock and sold the stock two days before they advised him to sell. In this case, the firm was more interested in its own welfare than in Steve's.

The right to have an investment fully explained to you. Make sure you understand every trade your broker makes on your behalf, the reason for the trade, and all the risks. When Mary Yamamoto requested that a broker who contacted her send her a detailed explanation of a limited-partnership investment, along with its prospectus, the broker hung up quickly and never called back. He couldn't deliver what Mary wanted and was trying to defraud her. Mary escaped this trap because she had made it a habit to insist that all verbal explanations from a broker be followed up in writing.

The right to total information. You are entitled to complete information about an investment possibility. This means that you should be informed about the bad points of the investment as well as the good ones. The only way an investor can make a valid judgment about an investment is by having all the facts. The seller/broker of a limited partnership must inform you that it is a long-term investment—perhaps seven to ten years—and that if you want to sell your interest before that time, you may receive only a small percentage of your investment back. If the seller/broker does not do this, you have not been fully informed. Similarly, if you are not told that a bond is callable (that it can be called in by the issuer prior to maturity), you have been deprived of some of the facts, and your rights as an investor have been violated.

The right to know what documents you are signing and why you are signing them. Investors should also keep copies of all papers they sign. Howard and Sylvia Fletcher thought it was standard operating procedure for their broker to ask them to sign a blank document. When the broker later filled in portions of the form erroneously with the direct purpose of defrauding them, they ended up losing more than $20,000, with no proof of misconduct.

The right to a full disclosure of the costs of any given investment. You should be told about all commissions, hidden markups, charges, and loads—and when and under what circumstances they are to be paid. You should also be told about penalties, maintenance charges, service charges, and redemption fees that might be incurred—and when they would be assessed. Because he was anxious to make a mutual-fund sale to Gil Levy, his broker failed to tell Levy that he would have to pay a large load when he was ready to sell the fund. Levy was particularly upset because he had asked the broker specifically about other fees and the broker assured him that there were none. By not fully disclosing *all* the costs, the broker had violated Levy's rights as an investor.

The right to be sold only "comfortable" investments. Every investor has a specific tolerance for risk. If you are conservative by nature and you depend on your investments for much of your income, you will feel much more comfortable with blue-chip stocks than with high-risk investments. You should not be sold any investment that doesn't match your risk profile. When retiree George Gifford, who was investing for income, was sold speculative penny stocks by an unscrupulous broker, Gifford's rights were violated.

The right to a good execution of a trade. You should expect a clean, uncomplicated execution of a trade that has been ordered. If any complications develop, it is the brokerage firm's fault, not yours. Jonathan Rawls placed an order to buy 100 shares of a $20 stock. When he failed to receive his usual confirmation five business days later, he called his broker. It seems that the order got lost and was never executed. Rawls missed the chance to realize a profit of $200 because the stock had risen two points since the day he had placed the original order. The broker-dealer was at fault.

The right to have your directions followed strictly and exactly. When you give directions to a broker, it is your right to expect that those directions will be followed. For example, if you direct your broker to put a stop loss on a stock you own, you have the right to have that order carried out exactly as you requested. A customer's rights have been violated if his broker neglected to sell his stock at $70 when he had specifically left a stop loss order with the firm at that figure and the order was ignored, resulting in much greater loss than the customer had sought to avoid.

The right to have accurate, up-to-date information concerning your brokerage account. Just as you expect a bank not to mark checks "insufficient funds" if in fact you have enough in your account to cover them, the same holds true for a brokerage account. In order to make informed decisions regarding your investments, you need to have up-to-date and accurate information about all your accounts. Robert Walsh was misled when his monthly statement showed that his account had less in it than it actually had. As a result, Walsh was unable to take advantage of a profitable opportunity that came up.

The right not to be sold more than you can afford. You shouldn't be "talked into" buying a security that will put you over your head financially or expose you to unexpected risks. Michelle Smith's financial adviser knew that Michelle was in bad financial straits, with only $2,000 left in the bank, yet he purchased for her 200 shares of a $10 stock. The broker convinced Michelle that this was a sure thing and that her $2,000 would double quickly to $4,000. He promised she would soon be back on the road to financial recovery. It was a risk she should not have been encouraged to shoulder.

The right to the truth. If, for example, a broker misrepresents his or her expertise to you, your rights have been violated. That's what happened when Derek Hogan's broker told him he was an expert in computer stocks, when in fact, he knew little about the industry.

The right to seek legal redress if a financial professional commits an act that results in monetary damage. Your ultimate remedy is to obtain total satisfaction when your broker has violated securities laws, rules, or regulations (see chapter 11).

What the Rights Mean

These rights not only spell out what you should expect as an investor but also can serve as a code of ethical behavior for registered representatives and broker-dealers. A violation of any one of these rights leading to a monetary loss is cause for invoking the final right—that of redress.

Your Rights as an Investor

In addition to your legal rights, you have the right to protect yourself. Among the things you should consider are the following:

Know with whom you are dealing. If you have never heard of a firm that wants to do business with you, you should request information on the firm's track record and its principals as well as on the qualifications of the individual with whom you will be dealing if you invest. Then you should double-check this information with the NASD (see chapter 9). If you receive a call from a broker who works for a firm that you have never heard of, check it out with your state's securities bureau. Similarly, get the name of the broker's branch manager and arrange for a face-to-face meeting. If the broker works for a distant firm, you may want to consider opting for a more local company that you can personally check out.

Pay a fair commission to a broker. Brokers, of course, are entitled to be compensated for putting the buyer and seller of a security together, and for their honest advice, but you should not be overcharged for this service. Brokerage commissions vary on different products. The standard commission on a stock or bond trade is normally not in excess of 5 percent of the value of the securities. But the commission on the sale of a no-load or low-load mutual fund may be less, or the commission on a limited partnership unit may be more. When Maggie Curtin, who had never invested before, paid a 10 percent commission to her broker for a stock purchase, she didn't realize that the broker and his firm were acting together to defraud her. It was only later, after she was contacted by regulatory authorities, that she was told she had been duped.

Choose a diversified portfolio. There is great danger in putting all of your eggs in one basket. It is safer to be diversified in stocks and industries. Because Barry Archer's broker sold Barry nothing but auto industry stocks, Archer's income fell when auto industry stocks fell and he had no other resources.

Do not be rushed into making a decision. An investment is not something that should be hurried. You should think long and hard about making any investment, and you should seek the advice of others if necessary. Herb Hamilton realized that the broker who called him out of the blue might be up to no good when he insisted Hamilton make a decision "right now" on an investment he was touting.

Know whether the seller or the seller's employer has any financial interest in the product being sold. This involves incentives, extra payments, exclusive management, or part ownership in the product. The rights of Ken and Eileen Nagy were violated when their registered rep failed to inform them that his employer was both the co–general partner and the exclusive sales agent for the limited partnership they had purchased. If a broker-dealer sponsors a new stock issue or manages his own mutual fund, investors must be informed of that fact.

Know how the financial professional is being compensated. Is the professional earning a commission from the sale of the product, and if so, how much? Does the seller advertise that he or she does financial planning for free? If so, that may mean the individual is earning a commission on a recommended product. When Barbara Dunhill's financial planner convinced her to buy a mutual fund, he failed to tell her that he was getting a commission from the investment company that manages the mutual fund. The planner had infringed on Barbara's rights as an investor.

Know in advance whether or not you can gain quick access to your money if you need it. How easily can you withdraw your own funds? How liquid is the investment recommended to you? These and other questions about the ability to gain access to your money are crucial and must be answered correctly and promptly. A savvy investor will also have questions about liquidity confirmed in writing.

Penny stocks generally have an established market based on the ebb and flow of supply and demand. However, if adverse information about the company comes to light, and the price of the company falls sharply, confidence in this security may cease to exist. In this case, no one will be interested in buying. Theoretically, you should have access to that invested money, but if there are no buyers, there can be no sale.

11 · HOW TO SETTLE OR FILE A COMPLAINT

Bringing legal proceedings against a broker may be an expensive and time-consuming process, and there is no guarantee that you will win your case. You should, therefore, make every effort to solve the situation before it gets to that stage.

Settlement Options

If you haven't lost money but you want to make a complaint against a broker or the firm, you can register that complaint with the District Business Conduct Committee of the National Association of Securities Dealers. The committee can bring an enforcement proceeding (a proceeding in which a punishment is leveled) against a broker-dealer who is guilty of misconduct.

If a broker or a broker-dealer has committed what you feel is a violation of your rights and you have lost money, your first move should be to contact your broker for an explanation. If the response is not satisfactory, your next step is to contact the broker's manager. Mail a certified letter, return receipt requested, telling your side of the story and asking if this matter can be resolved without resorting to legal action. You can also threaten to take the matter before the SEC, the NASD, the NYSE, or the state regulatory authorities. In some firms, brokerage managers have the responsibility for settling small disputes between brokers and their clients. Of course, some may play hardball and be unwilling to give an inch. However, branch managers are interested in keeping customers for the firm, and they usually don't want adverse publicity. Therefore, you may be offered a financial settlement after the matter has been investigated by the firm's compliance department. If the settlement is satisfactory and you accept it, the matter is resolved.

During this period, however, it is vital that you do as little communicating as possible with the brokerage firm. Just give them your version of what happened and nothing else. If you are asked for more information, such as a letter detailing the events as they occurred, or you are asked to produce your records, *don't do it,* because it may be used against you later.

If, after talking to the branch manager, the matter is still unresolved or the settlement offer is *not* acceptable, consult an attorney. But hiring an attorney may be an expensive proposition. Decide whether your loss is substantial enough to justify the expense. Although there is no precise rule of thumb, it is probably worthwhile consulting an attorney only if your loss is greater than $10,000.

You can file a complaint with the enforcement sections of the SEC, the NYSE, the NASD, the AMEX, or your local state securities department. These agencies can bring disciplinary action against a broker, but generally they will not resolve a dispute or help you get your money back.

If you have a claim of $10,000 or less, small-claims arbitration is available through the NASD, the NYSE, and other SROs. For a small fee, you can have your claim reviewed and decided by an impartial arbitrator. In most such cases, an attorney's fees are not warranted, and the case usually can be heard and decided in a relatively short time. For information about small-claims arbitration, call the NASD (202-728-8000 or 212-858-4000) or the NYSE (212-656-3000).

Arbitration

Unresolved disputes between investors and registered reps can be solved: by arbitration or by going to court. **Arbitration** has become the method used for the vast majority of cases. ·

Self-Regulatory Organizations

The SEC has given the securities industry the power to police itself by creating **self-regulatory organizations** (SROs), which are responsible for conducting arbitrations. All of the major and regional stock, commodities, and options exchanges are SROs. Actual jurisdiction of the SRO depends on the exchange in which the broker has membership.

Most arbitrators who hear disputes will accept nontechnical language. SROs also solve disputes between broker-dealers or between registered reps. SROs, then, function as umpires for the securities industry, no matter who the disputants are.

In addition to SRO arbitration, the American Arbitration Association (AAA) also provides arbitrators for securities arbitrations as well as for other types of disputes.

According to a recent survey,* customer claimants received some type of monetary award approximately 58.9% of the time when using AAA. Claimants using SROs recover at least something 56.1% of the time. It should be noted, however, that investors are not always legally entitled to arbitrate at the AAA.

Arbitration Clauses

Most forms and agreements that broker-dealers require their customers to sign contain a statement similar to this: "Any con-

*Source: *Securities Arbitration Commentator*

troversy arising out of or relating to this contract or the breach thereof shall be settled by arbitration. . . ." By signing this form, you waive your right to take complaints against the broker to court. This is known as an **arbitration clause.** When you signed any type of customer agreement, you probably agreed to arbitration, whether or not you were aware of it. Your other main choice in case of a dispute is suing in a court of law, and that forum is generally available only if you have *not* signed an arbitration clause.

If you refuse to sign a customer's agreement because of an arbitration clause, the broker-dealer can refuse to accept your account. Since the vast majority of broker-dealers require the signing of such an agreement, as a practical matter, you almost always must agree to arbitration if you want to invest.

Not all arbitration clauses are exactly the same. They may vary in terms of where an arbitration can be brought or the circumstances under which arbitration may be mandated. There may be differences in wording depending on the state in which the account is opened or on the broker-dealer involved. Nevertheless, the basic right to arbitration is offered in every state.

As a result of recent landmark U.S. Supreme Court decisions, nearly all investors who are seeking a monetary recovery from a broker-dealer *must* go to arbitration if they signed an arbitration agreement. As a result, very few cases wind up in court. These decisions, known as *Shearson v. McMahon* and *Shearson v. Rodriguez*, have already greatly increased the number of arbitrations, and many more can be expected.

Court decisions are still in flux on the issue of whether the investor has any choice as to which arbitration forum will be used.

Following Through

If you have lost money as a result of a registered representative's wrongdoing and you have not been able to settle with the broker-dealer, you (or, in some cases, your attorney) should file for arbitration.

Arbitration is significantly different from a court proceeding, where it can take several years before a case comes to trial. An arbitration proceeding usually can be heard in a year or less, and can be completed in just a few days of hearings. Because less time is expended, arbitration is frequently far less costly than a court case. Generally, both sides will pay fees to the SRO conducting the arbitration. An investor who is successful in the proceedings may have the fees refunded.

Most arbitrations are run by the three most important SROs—those of the NASD, the New York Stock Exchange, and the American Stock Exchange. Each SRO has a director of arbitration who schedules the arbitrations and assigns the arbitrators to each case. The NASD defines arbitration as "a method of having a dispute between two major parties resolved by impartial persons who are knowledgeable in the area in controversy." Arbitrators are, for the most part, individuals who have an intimate knowledge of the securities business. Judges and juries often do not have that same degree of expertise.

Arbitrators are classified either as *public* or *industry* representatives. Public arbitrators are not currently and were not recently employed in the securities industry. Industry arbitrators have a direct tie to the industry, as either present or recent employees. If the amount in dispute is $10,000 or more, two public arbitrators and one industry arbitrator will be assigned. If the amount is less than $10,000, one public arbitrator will be used. Decisions are rendered by a majority vote. Three-to-zero or two-to-one will decide an arbitration proceeding. Recent statistics show that *more than 50 percent of the time, customers who enter arbitration win their cases and recover some damages.* The deck is not stacked against you.

Arbitration Rules and Procedures

Although sworn testimony is taken, the rules of evidence are more informal and the procedures more relaxed in arbitration. This is one of the advantages of arbitration.

Proving Your Case

Proving and winning an arbitration case is not an easy matter. Proving a case may require analyzing trading strategies, suitability requirements, or the method of calculating commissions. Even in the simplest case, if you hire a lawyer, your lawyer may have to subpoena order tickets from the broker-dealer and get time and price information from the various exchanges involved in the proceeding.

In addition, copies of all exhibits are needed for each arbitrator, for the SRO, for the broker-dealer's attorney, and for yourself. You may need to hire an expert witness such as a CPA, another stockbroker, a finance professor, or a retired executive of a broker-dealer firm. You may also need to obtain back copies of *The Wall Street Journal* or other industry publications. You can find many of these in the library, but it may also be necessary to hire a professional researcher to search for information that can be found only in computer data bases. Depending on the part of the country you are in, an attorney will charge from $100 to $300 an hour or a contingency fee, or a combination of an hourly rate and a contingency fee.

Arbitration works for both brokers and customers. Brokers like arbitration because it saves legal costs and assures them of knowledgeable "judges." They also feel that if they have to pay, the verdict won't be reached by a "runaway jury" whose sympathies lie with the client.

Customers also like arbitration because it generally saves them legal fees. It is much speedier, and, because the procedures are more informal, the customer needn't worry that the case will be thrown out on some legal technicality. Once a decision is rendered, it is final and binding. Almost no appeals are allowed. This is attractive, because, with very rare exceptions, a wealthy broker-dealer will not be able to present appeals and thereby increase your legal fees while delaying paying a judgment.

Damages

In cases where registered representatives have committed flagrant, outrageous acts, an arbitration panel may award a wronged customer **punitive damages**—damages assessed to teach a lesson so that kind of behavior is not repeated. Punitive damages usually are awarded over and above the **compensatory damages** that are given to compensate for a loss. For example, if you lost $25,000 because a registered representative defrauded you, the arbitrators could award you the amount of loss you sustained plus a further $10,000 in punitive damages. Recent challenges to the investors' right to punitive damages in arbitration have been brought to court by broker-dealers. At this time, it is unclear whether investors will continue to have this right.

Failure to pay an arbitration award issued by an SRO is a violation of exchange rules, with the violator being subject to disciplinary proceedings.

Until recently, it was rare for arbitrators to award punitive damages, but that practice is becoming more acceptable as a greater number of cases are ending up in arbitration rather than in court. The decision on whether to award punitive damages and in what amount is purely discretionary with the arbitrators. The amount depends on how outrageous the arbitrators judge the offending conduct to be. However, punitive damages are still awarded in only a small percentage of cases, and only for the most flagrant conduct—such as when brokers have embezzled a client's money or have forged a client's signature on a document. In a few cases, arbitrators have awarded punitive damages in instances of churning, unauthorized trading, embezzlement, and forgery. Most awards are just for the actual losses.

The arbitration system is not perfect, and injustices occur from time to time. However, when you weigh its advantages against the cost and time involved in a lawsuit, you may be better off utilizing arbitration. The final decision whether to utilize arbitration or court should be made after obtaining legal advice based on the individual facts of your case.

Settlements

Many cases are settled before they reach arbitration or court. For various reasons, the broker-dealer may decide that it is better to settle a claim than to subject itself to the time, expense, and possibly higher award that might result from legal proceedings.

You have to decide whether or not to settle. If you agreed to pay your lawyer a contingency fee (a percentage, often 33 percent, of any eventual award), that agreement applies to settlement amounts as well as final awards. If you didn't agree on a contingency fee, you pay the attorney's hourly rate.

With a settlement, you can expect to get less than you are asking for. However, proper and equitable settlements are to be encouraged. Just because you bring a case doesn't mean you'll win, and even if the arbitrators do find in your favor, they may award you less than you asked for.

All settlements and awards of $5,000 or more must be reported to the SRO, which makes that information available to state regulators and others. As a result, a broker-dealer may be under some pressure from its registered rep who is subject to the reporting to settle for less than $5,000. Experienced securities attorneys know about this $5,000 reporting rule and will not let you be talked into accepting a lower amount if you are entitled to more.

Going to Court

If you have not signed an arbitration agreement somewhere along the line, you have the option of going to court to solve your dispute. But going to court is extremely time-consuming and expensive, so you may want to think of arbitration as your ultimate remedy. However, there are three advantages of going to court: (1) If you are on the losing end of the decision, you can appeal to a higher court; (2) you will be able to obtain more information during discovery (a pretrial disclosure procedure); and (3) you will be judged by a jury of your peers. However, some of these points also work to the advantage of your broker. It may pay to ask a competent attorney to help you make the decision on whether to go to court or to arbitration.

Role of the Attorney in Arbitration

Do you need an attorney to represent you in an arbitration proceeding? It is not legally required, but as a practical matter—yes. Even though arbitration is a simpler procedure than court, you still need an experienced lawyer who has represented clients in these situations and knows how the industry works.

Many unexpected things can occur during the arbitration hearing. For example, because the broker's career may be at stake, he or she may lie under oath. Experienced and savvy attorneys expect that and know how to handle it in cross-examination. In addition, securities lawyers know what documents to ask for in that preliminary phase of a case known as "discovery." Further, it may be necessary to call witnesses, such as branch managers, compliance officers, experts, and possibly even the registered representative to testify under oath. Many securities attorneys employ specialists who are expert at reading broker-generated computer data, which is vital in interpreting what actually occurred when a trade was made. These specialists can also decipher complicated confirmations and statements.

In short, your attorney must be a skilled trial lawyer with a specific familiarity with the securities industry and the way it operates. Just because you lost money doesn't mean that you have a case. It may be that the loss resulted from a sudden change in market conditions or some other external cause having nothing to do with the broker. Your lawyer must prove wrongdoing on the part of the broker, and that can be difficult.

Finding a Lawyer

Securities lawyers are specialists who work on investor-related cases. Most general legal practitioners know little or nothing about securities law and are not, therefore, good choices to represent you in a dispute with a brokerage firm. Here are some tips for finding a top-notch securities attorney:

• If you have a general attorney, ask for a referral.
• Ask your accountant for a recommendation.
• Call your local bar association and ask for a list of securities specialists. If you live in a rural or suburban area, you may be referred to someone in a nearby city, because securities lawyers tend to practice in urban centers.

Try to get at least three names. Interview each one before you make your choice. Here's what to ask:

• How many years has he or she specialized in securities cases?
• Does the attorney specialize in representing investors or securities firms? (There could be a conflict of interest.)
• Does the lawyer have time to work on your case? Since there are not many securities specialists, those who are available tend to have a large caseload.
• What kind of fee will you be charged? Consider negotiating the fee with the lawyer.

Fees

A lawyer who is convinced that you have a good case and that you will probably get a monetary award may ask for a contingency fee, which means the lawyer takes an agreed-upon percentage of any award you receive. Frequently that fee is one-third of the award. Some will insist on a higher percentage; some will accept less. Others may agree to negotiate the percentage. If you receive no award, your attorney receives no fee.

However, some lawyers may charge a flat hourly fee. Although these fees vary from one locale to another, you can expect to pay from $100 to $300 an hour.

There are also other fees that must be paid:

• Forum fees are similar to court costs. You pay a forum fee based on the damages you are claiming, the length of the arbitration, and the particular SRO you are using.

• If your exhibits are voluminous, the copying charges can run to hundreds of dollars.

• Expert witnesses' rates can run from $500 to $5,000 or even more, depending on the amount of time involved. However, not every case requires an expert witness.

• A professional researcher may charge hundreds of dollars.

The Best Defense Against Fraud

The American capitalistic system relies to a great extent on investment by individuals and institutions. Investors will continue to invest only if they have confidence in the system. Since individuals invest through a stockbroker, it is crucial that the conduct of stockbrokers and other financial professionals be governed by the rules of fair play and be monitored carefully. The securities laws, rules, and regulations provide guidelines for broker behavior and redress if violations occur.

Nevertheless, it is the investor who must be on the front line of the effort to stop the illegal practices of stockbrokers and other investment professionals, if and when they occur. Most stockbrokers and other financial professionals are honest. But—as in every area of consumer activity—knowledge, caution, and personal attention will help guarantee the best value for money spent and protect against rip-offs and fraud.

APPENDIX

Sample Forms

Power of Attorney—Limited—Authorization to Buy and Sell

┌─ STENCIL AREA

TO:

I hereby constitute and appoint _____
(whose signature appears below), my agent and attorney-in-fact, with full power and authority for me and in my behalf to subscribe, buy, sell (including short sales), and to trade in stocks, bonds, options or any other securities, limited partnership interests or investment and trust units, whether or not in negotiable form, issued or unissued, foreign exchange, commodities, and contracts relating to same (including commodity "futures"), on margin or otherwise, for my account or accounts with you, however designated, and whether presently open or hereafter opened.

You are accordingly authorized and empowered to follow the instructions of my said agent and attorney-in-fact in every respect with regard to any such subscriptions, trades, purchases or sales, long or short, on margin or otherwise, for my account, and I hereby ratify and confirm any and all transactions, trades or dealings effected in and for my account(s) by my said agent and attorney-in-fact, and agree to indemnify you and hold you free and harmless of any loss, liability or damage by reason thereof.

This power of attorney, authorization and indemnity is in addition to (and in no way limits or restricts) any and all rights which you may have under any other agreement or agreements between your firm and me, and shall inure and continue in favor of your present firm, its successors, by merger, consolidation or otherwise, and assigns.

This power of attorney and authorization shall continue in full force and effect, and you and your successors and assigns shall be indemnified in relying thereon, until you shall receive written notice of revocation thereof, signed by me; or in the event of the termination thereof by my death, or my mental incapacity, judicially determined, until you shall have received actual notice thereof, and such revocation or termination shall in no way affect the validity of this power and my liability under the indemnity herein contained, with reference to any transaction initiated by my agent and attorney-in-fact, prior to the actual receipt by you of notice of such revocation or termination, as above provided.

Dated at _____, this _____day of _____, 19 ____

WITNESS:		SIGNATURE OF CLIENT
SIGNATURE OF AGENT		
AGENT'S OCCUPATION		BOTH SIGNATURES IF JOINT ACCOUNT
NAME OF EMPLOYER IF ANY		
ADDRESS		
RELATIONSHIP IF ANY, TO THE GRANTOR OF THE POWER		
AGENT'S ACCOUNT NUMBER		

Typical Account Statement

Off	Account	AE	Balances	Opening
OXT	555555		Cash	169200CR
SSN	155-55-5551		Margin	00
	From To		Total (Excluding Short)	169200CR
Statement Period	NOV 1 NOV 30/86		Short	00

Portfolio

Priced Portfolio Value	6118750	Net Worth	5518750

Type	Settlement Date	Entry	Quantity	Description
1	1105	BOUGHT	1000	WTS ADVANCED NMR/SE5
				NET
				DHB AAP
1	1105	SOLD	1500-	XIOX CORP
				NET
				DHB AAP
				CUSIP NUMBER: 983905100
1	1118	BOUGHT	1000	UNITS CYTRX CORP 91
				NET
				PROSPECTUS ENCLOSED
1	1128	RECEIVED	4000	APPLIED CTL SYS INC
1	1128	RECEIVED	4000	WTS APPLIED CTL SY91
1	1128	DELIVERED	2000-	UNITS APPLIED CTL SY

QUANTITY	PORTFOLIO SUMMARY
1000	WTS ADVANCED NMR/S85*
4000	APPLIED CONTROL SYSTEMS INCORPORATED
4000	APPLIED CONTROL SYSTEMS INCORPORATED WARRANTS EXPIRES 1991
10000	CISTRON BIOTECHNOLOGY INCORPORATED
1000	CYSTRX CORPORATION UNIT 3 COM & 3 WTS CL A EXPIRE 1991
1000	SUNRESORTS LIMITED N V* CLASS A
1000	TOTAL HEALTH SYSTEMS INCORPORATED
500	XEROX CORPORATION*

PORTFOLIO TOTALS

Closing	Income	This Period	Year-to-Date
600000DR	Dividend	00	00
00	Municipal	00	00
600000DR	Other Interest	00	00
00	Total	00	00

Information

Available for Borrowing (Margin)   518100

Price or Explanation	Amount Charged To Your Account	Amount Credited To Your Account	Annual % Yield
8 5/8	862725		
4 5/8		693525	
6.00	600000		
EXCHANGED EXCHANGED EXCHANGED			

PRICE	VALUE	ESTM INCOME	%YLD
7.937	793750		
1.687	675000	00	.00
1.812	725000		
1.687	1687500	00	.00
6.250	625000	00	.00
6.250	625000	00	.00
7.500	750000	00	.00
4.750	237500	00	.00
	6118750	00	.00

Confirmation

We confirm the following transaction subject to the agreement on the reverse side hereof.

HOLD SECURITIES

Do not detach along this perforation—Return Part 2 (Blue Copy)

Transaction(s)	Trade Date	Office	Account	Type	C	FC No.
YOU BOUGHT	04/30/90			1	7	380

Quantity	Price	Description
30,000	97 1/4	UNITED STATES SER-A 2000 DTD YIELD 8.923MT DUE 02/15/2000

Total Quantity	Gross Amount	Commission/Sales Credit	St. Tax
30,000	29,175.00		

PD 04/30/90 SN 7000086

Please review this confirmation carefully. If you disagree with any transaction or the details of any transaction, you must notify the branch manager of the office servicing your account immediately of your objection. Failure to notify us constitutes your acceptance of the transactions.

Please retain this copy and return the duplicate with remittance and/or securities to the branch office servicing your account.

Payment for securities purchased and delivery of securities sold must be deposited with us by the due date.

CUSIP No.	Market Cap S/U PE	Due Date
	5 7 U	**05/07/90**
	Reference No.	Amount
TREASURY NOTES		**29,745.58**
2/15/1990		
Y		
08.500% FA 15		

/Bond Interest	SEC Fee	Service Fee	Total Amount
570.58			**29,745.58**

See reverse side
for important information

TMS 04/30/90

GLOSSARY

American Depository Receipts (ADRs). Tradable receipts of foreign corporations held in American banks. The owner of an ADR is entitled to all the dividends and capital gains just as if shares were held in a domestic corporation.

American Stock Exchange (AMEX). The securities exchange that transacts the second-largest volume of business among the organized exchanges. Most of the firms that are listed on the AMEX are small- to medium-size companies. Like its larger cousin, the New York Stock Exchange, it is located in New York City.

Arbitration. A method of settling disputes between brokers and customers. A panel of arbitrators is used, and any decision rendered by the arbitrators is final and generally unappealable.

Associated person. A broker who deals exclusively in the sale of commodities. A stockbroker can be both a registered representative for the purpose of selling securities and an associated person when selling commodities. Associated persons are employed by futures commission merchants, the commodities equivalent of broker-dealers.

Auction market. A market in which the prices for stocks and

126

bonds are determined by competitive bidding between floor brokers who act on behalf of buyers and sellers.

Blue-sky laws. State laws that regulate the purchase and sale of securities. State securities departments operate under blue-sky laws.

Bond. An interest-bearing financial instrument issued by a corporation or government agency, typically with a maturity of ten to thirty years. It takes the form of an IOU—that is, the principal amount of the bond must be repaid with interest within a specified period of time. A bond buyer essentially lends money to the issuer of the bond and the issuer is required to pay back the loan with interest. (*See also* Municipal bonds; Treasury bonds.)

Broker-dealer. A firm that employs brokers to buy and sell stocks, bonds, and other financial products on behalf of others, and that buys and sells securities for its own account.

Call. An option that allows the option holder to buy the securities underlying the option at a specific price on or before a set expiration date. (*See* Option; Put.)

Callable. Bonds that are redeemable by their issuer prior to their scheduled maturity.

Cash account. A securities account in which all trades are settled in cash.

Cash management account. A securities account that in addition to providing a means of trading also provides checking and credit card privileges, and often margin transactions.

Caveat emptor. Latin for "Let the buyer beware." It is the philosophy that everyone should adopt before investing.

Central Records Depository (CRD). A computerized data base detailing, among other things, the disciplinary records of individual brokers.

Chartered financial analyst (CFA). A professional designation given to individuals who have passed an examination testing their expertise in the area of financial analysis.

Chartered financial planner (CFP). Designation earned by financial planners who have passed a series of examinations and have demonstrated some expertise in the financial planning field.

Chicago Board Options Exchange (CBOE). A specialized exchange where only options are traded.

Churning. An abusive practice in which a broker overtrades a customer's account for the purpose of generating commissions.

Collateralized mortgage obligation (CMO). A mortgage-backed security that separates mortgage pools into different "tranches" or groups based on age until maturity.

Commission. The fee charged to the customer by a broker-dealer for executing a trade. This fee is paid for buying or selling.

Commodities. Tangible goods, such as agricultural products (including wheat, corn, and pork bellies [bacon]), precious metals, oil, gas, and cotton. When commodities are sold as an investment, they usually are sold as "futures," or for future delivery. (*See also* Associated person; Futures contract.)

Commodities Futures Trading Commission (CFTC). The body that regulates the sale and purchase of commodity futures.

Common stock. Ownership units in a corporation. Usually, common stockholders have voting rights—that is, they can cast ballots for the board of directors of the corporation and they are entitled to receive dividends if a dividend is declared. (*See also* Equity; Preferred stock.)

Confirmation. A document sent to the customer after every trade, detailing the particulars of the trade, including the price and commission.

Convertibles. A class of securities, such as certain preferred stock or convertible bonds, that is exchangeable for a set number of shares of another type of security, such as common stock, at a prestated price.

Corporate bonds. Debt instruments issued by corporations. These bonds usually are rated according to the creditworthiness of the corporation.

Custodial account. A kind of account in which one individual, usually an adult, trades securities on behalf of another, normally a minor.

Debenture. An unsecured corporate bond. Such a bond is backed only by the unencumbered assets of the corporation.

Debt service. The making of interest payments and matured principal on outstanding debt.

Discount brokerage. A broker-dealer that charges lower commissions than full-service firms but offers no research or investment advice. Its registered representatives, for the most part, are paid a salary instead of commissions.

Diversification. The spreading of risk in a portfolio by purchasing different classes and different types of securities.

Dividend. The earnings of a corporation that are distributed to common stockholders. The amount of the dividend is determined by the board of directors of the corporation.

Equity. The difference between the market value of securities in a portfolio and the debit balance (amount owed to the brokerage firm).

Execution. The actual carrying-out of a trade. This involves the matching of a buyer and a seller at an agreed-on price.

Federal National Mortgage Association (FNMA, or "Fannie Mae"). This quasi-governmental corporation purchases mortgages from lenders, repackages them as mortgage-backed bonds, and sells them to investors. Many of the mortgages that are bought by FNMA have government guarantees.

Fiduciary. A registered representative has this status. It is a legal relationship based on trust and unselfishness.

Financial supermarkets. Usually very large broker-dealers that offer financial products in addition to securities, such as mortgages, insurance, credit cards, and checking accounts. These are also known as one-stop financial centers.

Full-service brokerage. A broker-dealer that offers a full range of investment products, including research as well as trading.

Registered representatives who work for these firms are paid by commission based on the number and size of the trades they execute.

Futures contract. An agreement to either buy or sell a specified amount of a commodity or a financial instrument at a particular price on a stipulated date in the future.

Government National Mortgage Association (GNMA, or "Ginnie Mae"). The function of this governmentally owned corporation is similar to that of FNMA (Fannie Mae). It packages together mortgages it has purchased from private lenders and sells them to investors as an entirely new security known as a Ginnie Mae. The corporation itself differs from FNMA, which is a publicly owned entity; GNMA is owned by the federal government, specifically the Department of Housing and Urban Development (HUD).

Inflation. A rise in the prices of goods and services over a period of time.

Junk bonds. Bonds with high interest rates and low ratings, indicating very high risk. They are distinguished from investment-grade bonds.

Limited partnership. An investment group that purchases and manages a business enterprise for profit. The group is set up as a partnership with a general partner who manages the enterprise and limited partners or investors who invest in it but have no management function. The enterprise can involve real estate, oil and gas wells, cable television installations, or a host of other businesses.

Liquidity. The ability of an individual to convert assets quickly into cash. For example, in a money market fund that has a checking account, the owner of the security can obtain access to cash simply by writing a check. That is a highly liquid security. On the other hand, a piece of real estate is considered illiquid because it normally takes a long time to sell the asset and to convert it into cash.

Listing. Refers to the process by which a security becomes eligible to be traded on an exchange. The security to be listed must meet qualifications set by the exchange.

Load. A sales charge paid by the investor on the purchase of mutual-fund shares. The fee can run as high as 8 percent. If a mutual fund does not levy a sales charge, it is known as a no-load fund. Some mutual funds charge a fee when the investor redeems or cashes in the shares. This is referred to as a back-end load.

Managed account. A securities account in which the investor gives decision-making power over securities to a money manager.

Margin account. A credit account in which the investor borrows money from the broker-dealer in order to buy stock. Thus, the investor initially pays only a portion of the price of the stock. Such accounts are governed by Regulation T of the Federal Reserve Board.

Market order. The most common type of order, by which the customer requests the broker to buy or sell a security on the market at the best available price.

Market risk. Those risks that are common to all securities in a particular class (e.g., stocks) and reflect movements of the market generally. These movements cannot be controlled, so there is a risk to the investor regardless of the merits of the individual security chosen.

Markup. A legal practice whereby a broker-dealer who is a market maker in a security raises the sales price above its cost before it sells the securities to the public. The NASD Rules of Fair Practice state that markups generally cannot exceed 5 percent over a valid offer made for the security.

Money market funds. Mutual funds that invest in short-term instruments that are traded in the "money market."

Moody's Investors Service. A firm that rates securities, primarily bonds and stocks, and publishes its independent findings

,in a variety of reference books and loose-leaf services. It is a competitor of Standard & Poor's.

Mortgage pass-through funds. Mutual funds that invest in mortgages purchased by two quasi-governmental bodies, the Government National Mortgage Association (GNMA) and the Federal National Mortgage Association (FNMA). Monthly principal and interest paid by mortgage debtors is passed directly through to the investors.

Municipal bonds. Bonds issued by state or local governments. In most cases, the bondholder doesn't pay federal taxes on the interest earned; in some cases, the interest may be free of state and local taxes as well.

Mutual fund. A security that pools money collected from numerous investors and invests in other securities, such as stocks, bonds, or money market instruments. These funds are managed by investment companies.

NASDAQ. National Association of Securities Dealers Automated Quotation, the system used by the over-the-counter market to execute and report trades to the investing public.

National Association of Personal Financial Advisors (NAPFA). The nationwide organization of fee-only financial planners.

National Association of Securities Dealers (NASD). An organization established by the securities industry to police itself. Its members include all broker-dealers who trade on any exchange or on the over-the-counter market.

Net asset value (NAV). The market value of a mutual-fund share. The NAV is determined (usually daily) by dividing the market price of securities in the fund portfolio by the number of shares outstanding.

Net worth. That amount by which assets exceed liabilities. Broker-dealers usually require an individual investor's net worth to be at a minimum dollar level before they can qualify for certain investments, such as limited partnerships.

New York Stock Exchange (NYSE). The biggest and best-known securities exchange in the country. Also called the Big Board, it is the premier trading market for thousands of common stock issues. The great majority of stock trades made on a daily basis are transacted on the NYSE.

North American Securities Administrators Association (NASAA). The association for state securities regulators. Its primary function is to provide information for its members.

Open order. Also known as a good-till-canceled order. This is a buy or sell order that has not been executed because the security has not yet reached a designated price.

Option. A contract giving the owner the right to buy or sell an agreed-upon number of shares of a particular security at a fixed price within an established time period. There are two types of options—puts and calls.

Over-the-counter (OTC). (1) A security that is not listed or traded on any organized exchange. (2) A market in which trading takes place not on the floor of an exchange but rather by telephone or computer. Penny stocks typically are traded over the counter, but so are some larger, better-established stocks.

Penny stocks. Over-the-counter stocks that usually sell for $1 or less a share at initial offering. Penny stocks are for the most part issued by start-up companies or existing firms that have an unstable earnings history. For that reason, penny stocks are considered high-risk investments.

Portfolio. A term referring to the combined securities holdings of an investor. The portfolio may consist of nothing but stocks, bonds, mutual funds, real estate, another group of investment vehicles, or any combination of these.

Position. The totality of an investor's holding in one particular security. For example, if an investor owns 1,000 shares of IBM, that would be the investor's position in IBM.

Preferred stock. A class of corporate stock with a specified dividend. It has a preference in the payment of dividends, and in the event of a dissolution of the corporation issuing the stock, it has a preference in the distribution of assets above common stock but behind corporate debt. (*See also* Common stock.)

Price/earnings ratio (P/E). Also known as "the multiple." An analytical tool for investors, it is the current price of a stock divided by its earnings per share.

Proprietary products. Mutual funds, limited partnerships, and other financial products offered and managed by a single broker-dealer.

Prospectus. A written offer to sell securities. It is a disclosure document, detailing business plans and risks associated with the security, among other points.

Put. An option that permits the option holder to sell a specified number of shares of the stock underlying the option to a buyer at a specified price, on or before a set expiration date. (*See* Call; Option.)

Rating(s). An evaluation of a security based on certain stated criteria. Ratings are normally issued by independent agencies who perform the evaluation work. Typical agencies are Standard & Poor's and Moody's.

Real estate investment trust (REIT). A company that manages a portfolio related to real estate for its investors. These securities usually are publicly traded.

Registered representative. Also known as a broker or stockbroker. An individual who, by virtue of passing NASD examinations, can act as a middleman for customers who desire to buy or sell securities. For their work, registered representatives earn a commission.

Rules of Fair Practice. A body of rules and regulations established and enforced by the National Association of Securities Dealers (NASD). These rules are meant to regulate the professional behavior of all members of the NASD. A violation of these rules can result in a monetary fine for the member, or temporary or permanent exclusion from the securities business.

Securities Act of 1933. A historic piece of legislation that was enacted to prevent fraud, deceit, and misrepresentation in the sale of securities. It provides that all investors have adequate information with which to make rational investment decisions. This law also established the Securities and Exchange Commission, which oversees and regulates the securities industry.

Securities and Exchange Commission (SEC). The federal agency responsible for overseeing and regulating the securities industry. The SEC has turned over some of its authority for regulating the industry to self-regulatory organizations (SROs).

Securities Exchange Act of 1934. A companion act to the Securities Act of 1933. Among other things, it requires full disclosure for securities listed for public trading on securities exchanges.

Securities Investor Protection Corporation (SIPC). Similar to the FDIC, it is a corporation that insures the securities and cash in customers' accounts against the bankruptcy of the broker-dealers who are members of it.

Security. Any investment vehicle such as a stock, bond, or mutual fund that can be purchased by an investor. The public sale of securities is regulated by the federal and state governments by means of a large body of rules and laws.

Self-regulatory organizations (SROs). Bodies set up by the securities industry itself to enforce the rules and regulations that have been applied to the industry. SROs also conduct the arbitration hearings where investors can obtain redress against brokers and broker-dealers who have committed fraudulent, unethical, or illegal acts.

Selling short. A technique used by an investor who believes that the price of a particular stock will decline. An investor borrows stock from a broker-dealer and sells it, hoping to profit by purchasing and replacing the borrowed shares later at a lower price.

Settlement date. The date on which securities purchased in a brokerage account must be paid for, or the date on which securities sold must be delivered. It is usually five business days after the trade date.

Specialized brokerage. A broker-dealer that specializes in trading one type of investment product, such as penny stocks or options. The firm may charge a full or discounted commission, and any research offered is limited to the firm's area of specialization.

Standard & Poor's Corporation. A securities rating firm that independently evaluates stocks, bonds, and other investment instruments. It reports its findings on a regular basis in a number of publications.

Statement. A document prepared by the broker-dealer for the customer that records all the transactions in the customer's securities accounts during the preceding period of time. According to stock exchange rules, statements must be issued in any month in which transactions take place and at least once every three months.

Stock. *See* Common stock; Preferred stock.

Stock exchange. A physical marketplace where trades are made. Buy and sell orders are filled on an exchange by employees of broker-dealers who are members of the exchange. The best-known exchange is the New York Stock Exchange.

Stop loss order. A customer's order to a broker that sets the selling price of a stock below its current price. The order is to be executed if and when it reaches the lower price, but it will not necessarily be executed exactly at that price.

Suitability rule. A rule that provides that in recommending an investment, a broker take into account a customer's risk tolerance, financial situation, and needs.

Trade. In investment parlance, a purchase or sale of an investment product; a transaction.

Treasury bills (T bills). Government-issued securities that have maturities of one year or less. Because they are backed by the full faith and credit of the U.S. government, which issues them, they are considered to be safe, conservative investments.

Treasury bonds. Long-term debt obligations of the U.S. government. These debts are backed by the full faith and credit of the government.

Truth in Lending Law. A piece of legislation in which the lender of funds, as in a margin account, must disclose to the borrower the true cost of borrowing.

Underwriting. One of the functions of an investment banker. This firm will normally purchase an entire new issue of securities from a company seeking to raise money. The investment banking firm will, on its own or in syndication with others, sell or distribute the issue to investors at a price greater than it paid for the issue.

Unit investment trusts. A security similar to a mutual fund, with the difference being that the securities that comprise the portfolio are fixed and unchanging.

Zero-coupon bonds. Bonds that pay no interest but are sold at a steep discount from their face amount. The purchaser receives the full face amount when the bond matures. For example, a 10-year, $1,000 zero-coupon bond might be purchased at issue for $400. At maturity 10 years later, it will pay to the holder $1,000. However, no interim interest payments are made.

INDEX